PARADOXES AND PROBABILITIES

Books by Barclay Cooke

Backgammon: *The Cruelest Game* (with Jon Bradshaw)
Paradoxes and Probabilities: *168 Backgammon Problems*

PARADOXES AND PROBABILITIES

168 Backgammon Problems

Barclay Cooke

RANDOM HOUSE

New York

Library of Congress Cataloging in Publication Data
Cooke, Barclay.
Paradoxes and probabilities.
1. Backgammon. I. Title.
GV1469.B2C6   795'.1   78-57106
ISBN 0-394-50126-8

Manufactured in the United States of America
2 4 6 8 9 7 5 3
First Edition

To Kenny, Michaele and John

CONTENTS

1
OPENINGS

Since there is a finite number of opening moves, learn them by heart. Even in this aspect of the game, however, there is disagreement; experiment, choose those you prefer and play them with confidence. You should also determine how to reply to your opponent's openings. Naturally there will be variations in your play because of his roll, but in a short time you should be familiar with and know how to handle all of them.

The one basic early tactic which should supersede all others is to do everything in your power to make both five points—especially your opponent's—as soon as possible. Once having established this anchor, be loath to abandon it early, no matter how many blots the enemy leaves in his outer board. As long as you hold this point you can afford daring maneuvers.

Also remember that though both bar points are valuable, neither has anywhere near the impact of either five point, so if you have a choice, opt for the five point.

One further bit of advice: as soon as the first die is cast, try for the moment to forget the race and seek position by forming blocks against your opponent. This is backgammon's first great paradox. Basically, the game is a race around the board, but if you play with only that thought in mind, you will have little success.

1

Red has opened with a 4–1 by starting his nine and five points. White retaliates with double 4's, his best. There could hardly be a simpler position; the game has just begun. But already the subtleties are evident because there are several choices. They boil down to the following: (A) White can hit twice and make his four point; (B) He can make Red's five point and his own four point, hitting once. Which is better?

(B) simply cannot be wrong; it gives great balance and should be chosen whenever Red is the superior player. But if a gammon were vital – in a tournament, for instance, with the score 13 all in a 15-point match – it would be sound to adopt (A) and go for a knockout. Incidentally, making W4 is far superior to W9 because it drastically diminishes Red's chances of reentering.

This opening problem demonstrates how quickly an apparently simple choice can be very tricky.

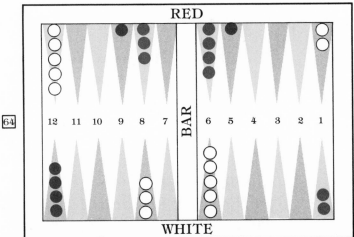

White to play 4–4.

2

There could scarcely be a simpler setup than this. There are many choices, of course, but all save two should be discarded: (A) make W7; (B) make W4. Though many would immediately make W7 without a glance at the other, (B) is by far the better play. White needs a good point in his board to offset Red's owning R5, and this roll secures it. In addition, White keeps an extra man on R12 which may be used to make the bar later.

The bar is a good point to have, but it is overrated in the early going. If you have a regular opponent and you both play about even, suggest to him that you'll play a series of alternate games, wherein every other game he gives you a 4–2 as an opening roll, and the next time you will give him a 6–1. He may think you're a patsy at first, but he'll soon discover that you've turned into a hustler.

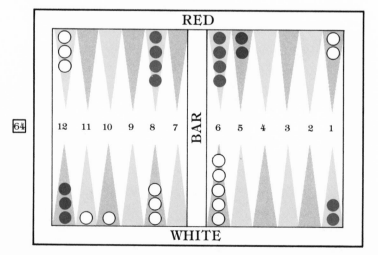

White to
play 6–4.

3 White would like to activate his back men, but has no good four. He would be too vulnerable if he split to R4 and started W4 or W9. Many players would break the twelve point, bringing two men down to W9 and W10, but to abandon the midpoint so early should be avoided if possible. The best play is to make W4 at the expense of W7. If Red rolls a six, he cannot improve his board as well, so White may be able to establish a forward point, and if Red does not get a six, White may remake W7. This 4 – 3 is a bad shot for White, but the key to the game is playing indifferent and difficult shots to the best advantage.

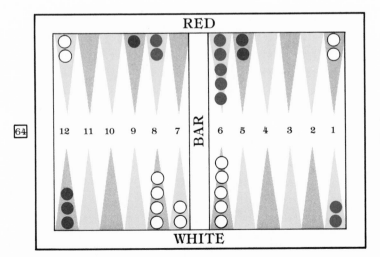

White to play 4 – 3.

4   Opening with a 4–1, White started his five and nine points, was hit with a 4–3 and now has rolled 5–4 from the bar. He has three choices: (A) he can make R5; (B) he can cover W9; (C) he can hit on W5. (B) should be rejected immediately. The nine point looks nice, but its value is negligible compared to R5. Beginners might tend to make W9 because the blot is eleven pips farther along than the one on R5. But even though it seems paradoxical, a sound principle to follow is: "As soon as the game starts, forget the race and seek position." This basic philosophy is demonstrated perfectly here. The correct play is to make R5 and go to work from there. You have established the most important defensive point on the board and are ready for any reply by your opponent. There is a case for aggressively hitting on W5, and an expert pitted against a beginner might attempt this, but never the reverse. In the vast majority of cases it is never wrong to dig in and make R5 in the early going.

  This concept is routine for most experienced players, but its importance cannot be overemphasized.

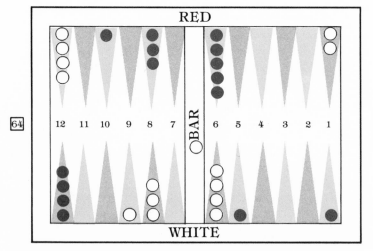

RED

WHITE

12 11 10 9 8 7 BAR 6 5 4 3 2 1

White to play 5–4. He is on the bar.

5 Here is a simple early position that takes some thought. White opened with 2 – 1 and started his eleven and five points. Red answered with 2 – 2 and elected to make W5, hitting. (Remember, even though conservative, this play by Red simply can't be wrong.) White rolled 6 – 1, entering and coming out to R7, where he was hit with a 5 – 1. Now, how should he play his 2 – 1?

I'm sure that over 95 percent of all backgammon players would enter on R1 and cover W11, blocking sixes. I won't go so far as to say that this is incorrect, but my instinct rebels against it; it would be much better to make R2, leaving W11 and R1 open. Red needs a six to cover R7, and White increases his own chances of making a forward point in Red's board by this play. In addition, if Red chooses to break his W5 anchor and hit with a six, White has a potential back game.

I like positions where I feel strongly that a certain play far outweighs another more obvious one. Here is such a situation. I would make R2 against any type of player, and in any money game or tournament, regardless of the score, and I would welcome my opponent piling three men on his one point in order to block W11, a point that I certainly don't want.

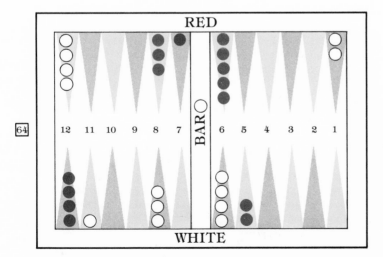

RED

BAR

64 12 11 10 9 8 7 6 5 4 3 2 1

WHITE

White to play 2 – 1. He is on the bar.

6 Here is an early position which demonstrates basic tactics. No matter how short a time you have been playing, it is not too soon to grasp the purpose behind the correct move here. Red opened with a 2–1 and started his eleven and five points; White replied with a 4–2, hitting on R5 and starting W11. Red then rolled a 5–1, entering on W 5 and hitting on R5. So far the play by both sides has been correct. Now White has a 2–1 to play from the bar. It would be tidy to enter on R1, securing an anchor, and then covering W11, blocking sixes; after all, White is slightly ahead in a race. But here is a good time to follow the paradoxical backgammon adage: "In the beginning forget the race and seek position." You can worry about the race later when both armies are free of each other and there is no more contact.

To play R1 and W11 with this 2–1 seems natural in the early stages, but see how little such a move accomplishes. It gives Red complete freedom, making almost any number he rolls playable. Note that he can secure W5 with a four and make R5 with any six, three or one; thus, he has a good chance to do both on his next roll. What White must do here is to enter on R2 and hit on W5. By this play he tends to keep Red off-balance and hinder his making points because he must use part of his roll to reenter. Specifically, White diminishes Red's chances of making either five point.

In blot-hitting contests like this the player who rolls the first good double usually secures an advantage. Don't worry about this; simply try to understand the strategy back of this play. It is a simple maneuver for the expert, and is even becoming routine for most intermediate players, so much has the general caliber of play improved.

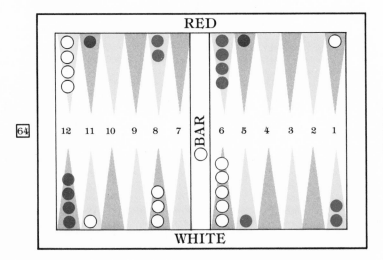

RED

64

12 11 10 9 8 7 BAR 6 5 4 3 2 1

WHITE

White to play 2–1. He is on the bar.

This problem will be of inestimable value if it persuades the novice to abandon the obvious, safe play in similar situations. To use a math analogy, the tyro will have graduated from algebra to geometry overnight.

7

It is early and White has options. He can hit on W10 or cover W5, but not both. The reason for including this problem is to point out the necessity of considering every angle. Too many would vacillate here between either of the above plays when they should quickly reject both and, instead, make R5. What can Red do now? Nothing. There is no number that can hurt White at this juncture if he makes his opponent's five point.

It would be bad advice to suggest that you shouldn't always be thinking when you play, but if there is an exception, it is in the early game when you have a chance to make the enemy five point. Don't even consider any alternatives; simply secure that bastion and you will be right infinitely more often than wrong.

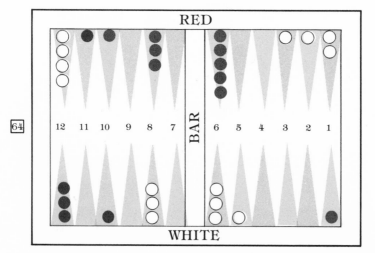

64

White to play 3 – 2.

8

White has no better one than hitting Red on W5. He is far ahead in the race at least for the moment, since Red has four men back. This being so, the natural inclination is to play conservatively; "When ahead stay ahead" is usually a reasonable philosophy.

Therefore most people would save the blot on R10, leaving only one man exposed. However, this would be wrong. The game is anything but a straight race, and White needs position badly. By boldly starting W11 he gambles, but the potential rewards are well worth it. One of the dangers of such a play is being hit twice, but Red cannot hit twice and also cover R5 (unless he rolls double 3's). To run for cover here before the battle is truly joined would not only be cowardly, but would also show lack of concept and insight. White should plunge in with both feet here and slug it out.

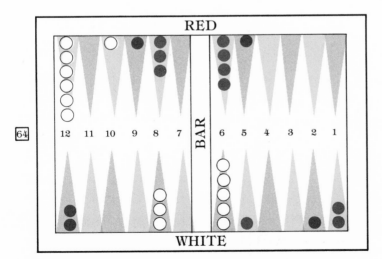

White has
2 – 1 to play.

9
There is nothing complicated about this position, even though White has several options. He can hit twice, cover R5 and bring a man over to W8, hit on R7 and continue to R12, or cover R5 and hit on W3 from W8. It is all a matter of priorities. If White is a beginner and race-oriented, he will probably grasp this opportunity to send a fourth R man back by hitting on R7. Such a play accomplishes little, however; White has no position, and to be far ahead in the race at this juncture means nothing. No matter what the score is, and whether it is a tournament or money game, it is sound tactics to make R5 with the two. This play is the cheapest insurance policy for whatever the fates hold in store for White. The five is optional and relatively unimportant; either move to W8 or hit on W3, but dig in on R5 and don't be lured away from there until the right opportunity presents itself.

There may be one exception to the above suggested move. If an expert is pitted against a newcomer, and the score is 13 – 13 in a fifteen-point match, it would be reasonable for the expert to hit twice on R7 and W3, trying to gain a tempo if Red should now roll any six and no three. But under all other conditions White should make R5. The strength of this anchor has been mentioned before; it is impossible to stress its importance too strongly.

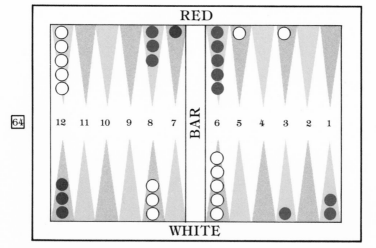

White to
play 5 – 2.

10 Here is a relatively simple early position. Red has his four point and leads in the race, but White has R5. Note once again the almost priceless value of this point. White's reflex action would be to make W7, but consider how he strips himself by this maneuver. His bar is a good point, but it looks stronger than it actually is in this position. He could also make R7, but since it would cost him R5, this play, though reasonable, should be rejected. He can't move the man on R2, so the only alternative left is to go from R1 to R9. White's timing is suspect, and this play tends to rectify it. If hit, he is delayed; if not, he has released a man to help shore up his front position.

The point to realize here is that because White holds R5 he has many options. He doesn't have to make the obvious W7 which constricts him; he can afford to be much more aggressive and to leave three blots around the board.

This problem shows the importance of timing; try not to strip yourself unnecessarily. Also, for the umpteenth but not last time it proves how difficult it is to overemphasize the importance of owning your opponent's five point.

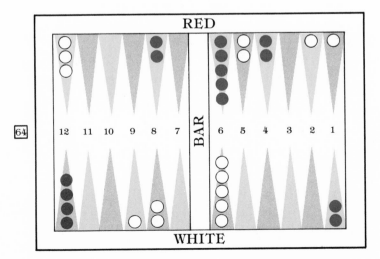

RED

64

12 11 10 9 8 7 BAR 6 5 4 3 2 1

WHITE

White to play 6–2.

11

The pivotal point coveted by both sides is White's four point. If Red secures it, White's advantage, though White is far ahead in the race, is gone. Therefore he should hit Red on W4 with the two, ignoring for now the blot on R11, and play the one from W6 to W5. Such a move is basic but, in the early stages of learning, seems unnatural and risky. But ask yourself this: if you know for sure that one of Red's dice on his next roll would be a four, wouldn't you still hit in the board to prevent him from establishing this important point? You should! Try to master this concept; it occurs constantly and costs heavily in the long run when not understood.

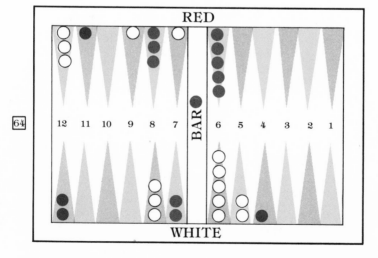

RED

64 12 11 10 9 8 7 BAR 6 5 4 3 2 1

WHITE

White to play 2 – 1. Red is on the bar.

12

White opened with a 6 – 3 and boldly started his ten and seven points. Red replied with 2 – 1, and correctly started R11 and R7. Ordinarily R5 should be slotted instead of R7, but not here; White needs a six to cover W7, and it would be a mistake to leave him a four shot in this position. Even though there have been only two moves, the duplication principle is already being illustrated. Now White rolls double 2's. This is a splendid early shot, and he should not squander it. He should immediately reject making W7 or hitting on R7. Of course he would like to do either or both, but he must realize that double 2's can be used to far better advantage. He has two sound plays: (A) make R5 (to make your opponent's five point early just can't be wrong); the other play (B) would be to make W4 and R3, which is more flexible and perhaps even better if White is the stronger player. The four point has great value now, and making R3 diminishes the strength of R7. Either play is strong and gives White a definite edge.

This problem shows how important it is to resist making obvious moves. Much of backgammon is either hitting or covering, but here both are wrong and give way to a more important priority.

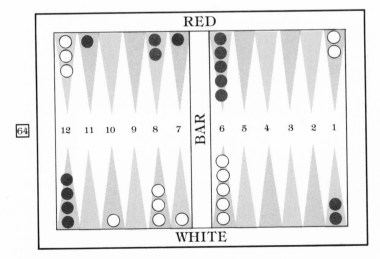

White to play 2 – 2.

13

Red has the early advantage and White must be aggressive. To enter on R1 and save the blot on W7 is unthinkable. White should try for R5 by entering there, and he might as well go all out by starting W5 with his one. This is risky, but if Red rolls any five or six — and he is favored to do so — he will be unable to hit twice, thus giving White an opportunity to establish a playable position. Moreover, even if hit twice, White has an open board on which to enter.

The value of not splitting one's back men too early is shown here. Even if Red should roll double 3's or double 1's and White stays on the bar he cannot be blitzed. To play this 5–1 conservatively would be weak and a losing proposition in the long run. There are occasions when you should quietly play a conservative waiting game, but this position demands boldness and daring.

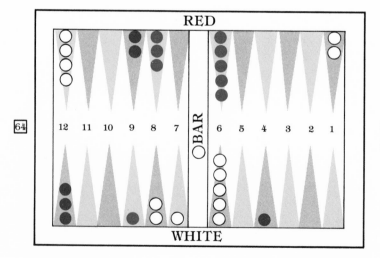

64

White to play 5–1. He is on the bar.

14

Throughout most backgammon games there are shifting critical goals. Here is an early example. What Red wants badly is R5. White realizes this, of course, and was hoping for a four in order to hit Red's blot there. Here is where many players would go wrong by putting R5 out of their minds for the moment and looking around for a way to build their own board. Splitting to W5 with the one and bringing the five to W8 creates several builders for the bar or W4, so they would opt for this aesthetic move. But by this play White only takes the pressure off Red. White should concentrate on the crucial spot, not divert his attention to irrelevant areas. To split to W5 with the one is fine, but he must hit Red on W1 with the five. By so doing he drastically curtails Red's chances of making R5. If White doesn't hit here, Red will be a 2 – 1 favorite to cover R5, but by being hit he becomes almost a 9 – 5 underdog. White has drawn first blood by securing W5, and this gives him an enormous edge in any hitting contest. He must exploit his superior position and try to keep Red off-balance. Right here he has an outside chance for a knockout. Notice, for example, what a return 6 – 2 would do to Red! Then compare how Red would play 6 – 2 if not hit; of course he would secure R5.

Earlier we mentioned shifting critical goals. If Red is lucky enough to make R5 despite W's play, the next goal might then become either bar point, and thereafter either four point. Try always to be aware of the immediate priority. To build lovely sand castles out in the desert may be fun and aesthetically pleasing, but it won't win backgammon games.

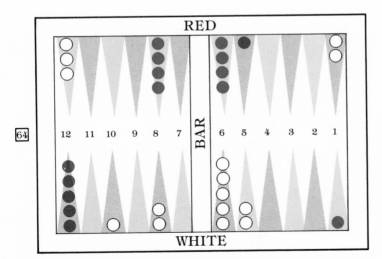

RED

64

12 11 10 9 8 7 BAR 6 5 4 3 2 1

WHITE

White to
play 5 – 1.

15

The game is just beginning, White having opened with 6 – 1 to make his bar, and Red answering with double 3's, making W4 and R5. This double gives Red a definite lead; already he is much better placed than his opponent. How then should White use his 3 – 1 to best advantage? W5 is valuable, but since Red has W4, it is hardly worth breaking W8 to make it. To advance both men in Red's board is too aggressive; White has no defense and such a move invites disaster, for Red could destroy him with even numbers. An alternate daring play, which has merit, though some might consider it foolhardy, is to start both W10 and W5. Combination sixes (2 – 2, 4 – 2, 3 – 3) are blocked, so only twenty shots hit, not twenty-four. Also, both sixes and ones are needed to make R7, a point that Red wants. A compromise not quite as risky would be to start W9, leaving a 5 or 4 – 1, thirteen shots. But this does not activate one of those extra builders on W6 which White must put into play as soon as he can. (Incidentally, even though White has the worst of it, he must not compound his problem by making the safe but aimless move W6 to W2. Always try not to put men out of action at any time, early or late. Sometimes it is inevitable, but far more seldom than it is done.)

The more one examines the position, the more starting W10 and W5 seems best. If Red fails to hit, White may be able to cover either or both of these blots and form a block of his own which will allow him more time to release his back men.

An interesting sidelight to notice here is the exceptional strength of an opening 3 – 3. White had the first move and started with two of the best shots he could ask for (6 – 1 and 3 – 1); yet due to Red's double 3's White would gladly begin the game over.

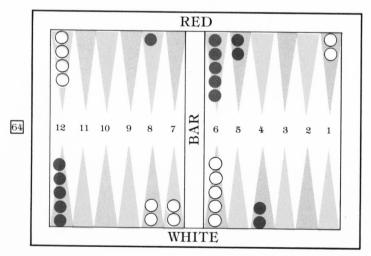

White to
play 3 – 1.

2
THE
MIDDLE
GAME

It is this part of the game, where the war is fought in the trenches or in a toe-to-toe slugging match, that is most difficult. It requires a sixth sense, instinct, insight, and the ability to improvise continually. Countless positions arise which look alike but are not at all and require different handling due to other subtle factors. There is no way to teach middle-game strategy; it can be absorbed only by experience. The timing of both sides, and when to hit or not, become vital. To add to your problems, no matter what plan you have made, at any instant the dice may render it obsolete. It is in these circumstances that the expert shows his mettle by adjusting, improvising and trying another tack. This aspect of back-gammon is why there is a case for arguing that it is the most impossible game to master.

No matter how good you become, two important facts remain. First, you will never learn it all; secondly, you will never have complete control over your destiny. Respect the dice, and learn to accept whatever they show. The vast majority of losers curse their luck and blame bad dice, but I suspect that fully three-quarters of them lose because of their bad play; they need far better dice than their opponent merely to break even. Be honest with yourself and try not to rationalize your losses; by so doing you will keep an open mind and can constantly improve.

16

Red has by far the better development, but this 6−1 keeps White in the game. He is still not well off, no matter how he plays it, but he shouldn't drop if doubled. (Probably there will be arguments about this, but I'd take the double in all money games and in most tournament situations.)

In any case, how should White play this roll? He has only two choices: the bar or W5. There is a school, rapidly gaining favor, which stresses the value of keeping one's builders diversified. There could hardly be a more worthwhile objective, but there is also a time-proven axiom which says that the five point is far superior to the bar, especially in the early going. If White makes the bar he has a valuable extra builder for his five point; sixes, threes and ones all will be working. But if he makes his five point, only sixes and ones make his bar.

I know that the "builder school" will violently disagree here, but to me the five point far outweighs the importance of that extra builder. I would make W5 with confidence, and would be delighted if in the same position my opponent chose to make his bar.

To be adamant about any facet of the enigmatic game of backgammon is ridiculous; I have changed my mind before and continue to do so all the time. But though many experts will disagree, I remain unconvinced that the bar is superior to the five point in such a position.

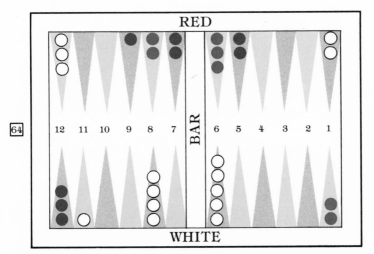

White to
play 6−1.

17

There could hardly be an easier problem than the playing of this 4 – 1, but there are two aspects worth discussing.

First, you have been correctly taught to make a point in your opponent's board for defensive purposes as soon as possible. If this reliable tactic has been inculcated in you strongly enough, you might be tempted to play the one to R2. It would create an anchor, and in the short run it could be correct. For instance, Red might roll a 1 – 4, enter and be unable to hit. Then if White countered with double 5's he'd be a hero — but a vulnerable one, should he employ such maneuvers regularly. Of course he must leave those men separated so that he can escape with both sixes and fives. In order to give himself the best diversification, White should move the four to W4 and the one to W5. Thus he has fours, threes and twos working on W1, and the two high numbers to escape.

Further, if Red fails to enter on his next roll, White has a great double here. He is far from home and there are possible diaster shots — especially double 4's and double 3's — but from Red's point of view it is a difficult take. In most tournaments Red would drop, and who could blame him? But once again I must emphasize that if you are Red and a beginner against an expert, you should take. Gamble on his getting a horror shot, or on your rolling a 6 – 1. The leverage gained by owning the cube cannot be stressed too strongly, and if the game should turn, as it often does, redouble boldly. If the dice favor you and you win a gammon, you will not only have buttressed your score but will have dealt your opponent a psychological blow from which he may not recover.

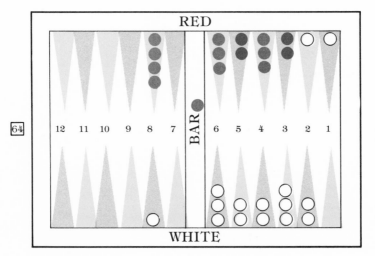

64

12 11 10 9 8 7 BAR 6 5 4 3 2 1

RED

WHITE

White to play 4 – 1. Red is on the bar.

18

Here is a simple early position. White is well ahead in a race, but his timing is bad. Especially awkward are his two men on W1 – unless, of course, he can reduce the game to a straight race. Here is a great opportunity to make a run for it. He should play both men off R7 to R10 and R12, leaving a three or five shot. The three may be needed to cover R5, and if he rolls any even number he cannot both hit and cover. In fact, he is more than 3 – 1 not to do so because double 1's can't hit.

Usually in positions like this the quality of the players is an important factor. If White is playing a more experienced opponent, he should jump at this chance to run, whereas if the roles are reversed the expert would be averse to breaking contact, thereby taking all the skill out of the game. If White risks this play and gets away with it, he can probably force Red to drop on his next turn by doubling. But here, no matter what White's skill, the best play is to run for it before Red improves his board and makes such tactics too dangerous. Unless Red gets one of his eight perfect shots, it will be dangerous for him to hit, but he virtually has to because he is so far behind in the race.

There is nothing difficult or brave about the suggested play; all that is required is the awareness that because of many factors now is the time to bolt.

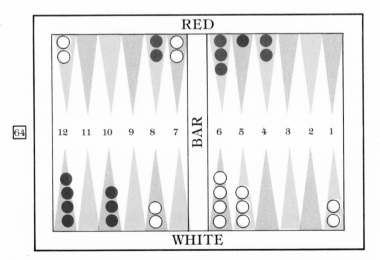

White to
play 5 – 3.

19

Red is obviously off to an early lead; he has both his five point and bar, plus three of W's men trapped in his board. White has two options: (A) either make W4, leaving no blots; (B) make W5 with the one and start W4 with the four. Since Red is far ahead already, it would be natural for White to decide on the more conservative (A), but (B) is much the stronger move. It not only secures a better point, but gives White flexibility; if he is hit on W4, White may make a second point in Red's board and be well placed to play a back game. Red's timing is reasonable, but he is stripped in his outer board and may have to advance too fast. If Red does not hit, White may then make W4 and opt for a blocking game. Sometimes slotting a man on your bar or in your board, even if correct, entails great risk, but here the risk is minimal because White will not be severely hampered if hit. To make the suggested play is not difficult once the position has been analyzed.

Look at it this way: save for double 3's, there is hardly a shot that Red could roll which would make (A) superior. If you considered (A), then rejected it and chose (B) without knowing exactly why, you are on your way to developing a feeling for this game. Here is an example of using your instinct, which you must continually develop to succeed. Countless situations arise all the time which are far more complicated than this one, so that sixth sense provides a big edge.

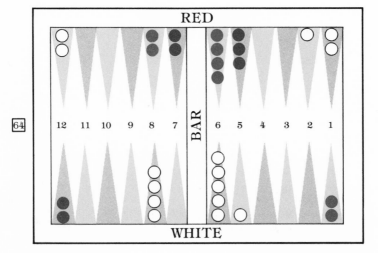

White to
play 4 – 1.

20   The decision whether to double or not here depends on many factors. There is no way you can expect a clear-cut answer without supplying several other details. For example, in a tournament match between an expert and a comparative beginner, the beginner should double, but not the expert, unless he is sure that his inexperienced opponent will drop. It is a "leverage" situation in that the threat of a gammon is serious—just what the tyro wants to offset his opponent's skill. On the other hand, if White rolls a four or a two he can't do much damage, even if he hits Red on the five point.

In a chouette or money game nobody could fault White for doubling. There is a definite chance for a gammon, and a position which would intrigue anybody with a gambler's instinct. Conversely, Red should take because he can turn the whole position around with one roll. Assume that White fails to hit on R5, and that Red secures this point with a one. Now he will have a five-point block and, in addition, will own the cube, which will exert pressure on White for the rest of the game.

To return to tournament play, if the score is 11–11 in a fifteen-point match, regardless of the relative skills of the opponents White should double and Red should drop. It is too dangerous to risk the match on this gamble. However, if this is the first game Red should take with gusto.

This problem only scratches the surface in demonstrating the 1,001 variations inherent in the doubler.

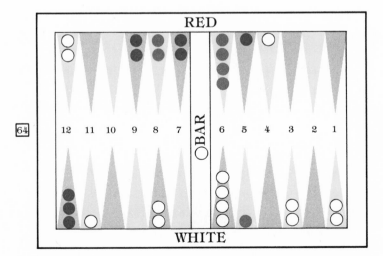

White to roll from the bar. Should he double?

21

White has been doubled early, and is in bad shape because he has no board and R has fine development. He enters on R1 and now must decide on his six. He has three choices. He could start his five point or either bar (to go to W2 is senseless). Coming out to R7 is foolhardy, yet starting W7 or W5 isn't appealing either. A decision like this is the essence of backgammon. Anyone can make his five point on an opening 3 – 1, but the skillful player, like the expert golf pro, plays his best when in a tough spot.

The correct play here is to start W5. The man on R1 is comparatively safe, and if White is hit on W5, he has a chance to secure an anchor in R's board. Also, fours are duplicated; that is, Red may need a four to make his bar. If Red does make his bar on his next turn, White will be favored to cover W5, and even though he has a man trapped back on R1, he will have excellent timing and a playable game with those three men of Red's on W1. W5 is preferable to W7 because it's a better point if not hit and because it is safer, being vulnerable to only fifteen shots instead of seventeen. Lastly, White wants to leave as few blots as possible.

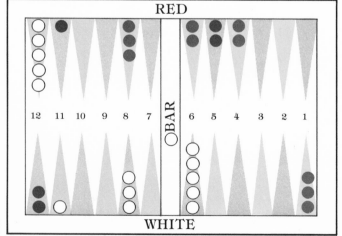

White to play 6 – 1. He is on the bar.

22 This could hardly be a simpler problem. White is forced to enter on R2 and has his choice of two sixes. Both are extremely awkward. He has been told, quite rightly, not to break his midpoint early. But the value of a forward anchor, like the one he holds on R5, has also been drilled into him. Which rule should he break? One of them must go.

Almost anyone who has been exposed to backgammon at all will play this correctly. White must start W7 and hang on to R5. First, the midpoint, though valuable, is not quite as important now that White has R5 rather than R1. Secondly, if White breaks W5 now he could be wiped out; 1–1, 2–2, 3–3, 4–4, 3–1, 4–1 and 4–3 all would be devastating. Thirdly, if White starts W7 he is still in the game, no matter what Red rolls.

Why include such an easy problem? The answer is to emphasize in graphic form the priceless value of your opponent's five point. Advertising people say that bombarding the viewers over and over again succeeds in selling their product. If keeping R5 has been presented in such a way that the reader learns the lesson once and for all, its inclusion is worth far more than the cost of this book.

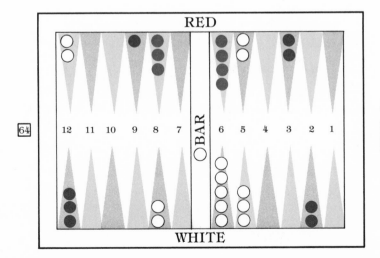

RED

64

| 12 | 11 | 10 | 9 | 8 | 7 | BAR | 6 | 5 | 4 | 3 | 2 | 1 |

WHITE

White to play 6–2. He is on the bar.

23

If anyone doubts that there are subtleties hidden in the cube, let him look at this position. Without further details, the question of whether White should redouble is unanswerable; it's yes in some cases and no in others. If you are White and a novice, pitted against Red who is an expert in a tournament match with a long way still to go, don't hesitate for a second to redouble. What leverage you have! He will see that 6−2 in his imagination costing him eight points, and most likely will drop. If he takes, don't be dismayed just because you have very little time. This is a great chance for you to offset his superior technique. Any time you can come to grips with your opponent on your own terms rather than on his, do so. He would like to wear you down with single, one-point games, so your tactics should be the opposite; escalate that cube every reasonable chance you get. Be ready when these opportunities occur; you can put the fear of the devil into a top player by such play.

Now for the negative. If the roles were reversed, all experts would know enough *not* to redouble here or they'd hardly qualify for being in that class. If you are Red and a comparative beginner against an expert who tries to bluff you out by doubling, take and redouble him to eight immediately unless he rolls a two or double 1's on his next roll. In positions like these the tyro has a big advantage, and he must use his leverage. Take advantage of the arrogance of your expert opponent; sometimes in such positions he will elect to drop, when from a mathematical view he has much the best of it.

There is an added psychological factor here; if you double and accept boldly in positions like this, you alert your opponent to the fact that he isn't playing a patsy; it's important to let him know that he can't boss you around.

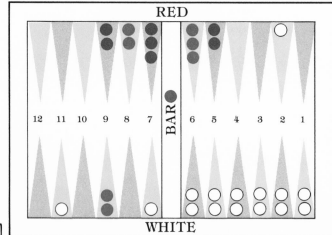

Red is on the bar. Should White redouble?

The principal reason for including this problem is to make the player aware of his opportunities in tournaments. In a money game the decision is far simpler; if I were Red I'd take the double every time but would not redouble unless I was convinced that White would drop.

$\mathcal{24}$ White rolled an early 5 – 5 and is trying to blitz Red. Each side has a man on the bar, and Red has his hands full trying to establish a defensive point. This 4 – 4 is a tremendous shot for White. He has already doubled and should go all out for a gammon. He enters on R4, hits a second of Red's men on W4, and then pauses to consider his final two fours. His primary objective is to prevent Red from securing *any* point in White's board. How best to accomplish this? Bring a builder to W10 from R7? Make W9? But what if Red rolls a two? He will then have an anchor and the chances of a blitz are gone. What White must do here is most unnatural; he should temporarily give up W6 to make W2. Many will howl with indignation; but consider Red's plight. White has a three-point board — an upside-down one, to be sure — but this is a situation where quantity, not quality, of points is vital. Never mind the order in which the board is made in positions like this. Unless Red rolls a four or a big double, he is going to be hard pressed to avert a shutout.

This is another example of priorities. From White's point of view, everything is secondary to stopping Red from establishing a point. If he is left alone on W2, he has an 11 – 25 chance of thwarting White, and he must not be allowed to catch his breath.

To project White's offensive tactics one step further, if Red rolls a 5 – 2 next time, entering one man and White then gets a 6 – 2, White should hit on W5, leaving two blots. There should be no halfway measures here; swing from the floor with everything you've got.

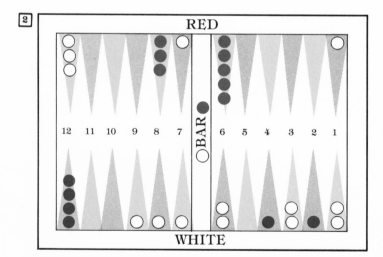

White to play 4 – 4. Both he and Red are on the bar.

25 A 3 – 2 might have been better, but White is not complaining. He covers W2 with the one, and now must decide on the four. It is natural to make W7 and be completely safe. But though there is risk involved, now is the time to break R7, while Red is on the bar and confronted with entering a five-point board. Admittedly this play leaves four blots exposed and, like any daring move, could prove a disaster. If Red entered and hit, and White failed to enter Red's three-point board, he would have to drop the redouble or be in danger of losing a gammon if Red decided not to double and go for one. Nevertheless, this is clearly White's best play. Twos and sixes are duplicated, so only six shots hit (5 – 6, 5 – 2 and 5 – 1). White is therefore a 5 – 1 favorite not to be hit, and should Red fail to throw a five, White will be well-placed to hit on W5 and be a strong favorite to win a gammon.

It is difficult to state with certainty what the single most important aspect of backgammon is, but near the top is the ability to see clearly when voluntary risks should be taken. There are several examples throughout this book, and they have been picked to attempt to induce in the reader a frame of mind that is ready and unafraid to play this way when the circumstances warrant it. Just because they backfire now and then is no reason to abandon them. On balance you will be far ahead if you continue to give yourself your best chance to win the game in which you are involved. In countless instances — and this is one of them — it is a crime to run for cover too soon, because you will probably have to pay dearly later for doing so.

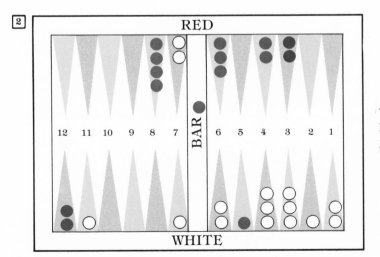

White to play 4 – 1. Red is on the bar.

$\mathcal{26}$ Here is a variation on a familiar theme: whether or not to risk being hit voluntarily when there is a reasonable, safe move. White can add a builder to W5 or he can make the more daring play to R9.

When decisions like this occur, White must appraise his position and that of his opponent accurately. Red owns a vital forward anchor on W4, while White has two men far back on R1. To have a builder on W5 is valuable in case Red decides to make a break for it, but White should note that Red has an extra man on W12, and there is hardly a roll which would make Red choose to leave a blot on W4. The timing of both sides is about even, so when every factor is considered, White should come to the conclusion that now is the time to make a run for it. At least Red has no builders inside his board, so White may recover even if Red hits him on R9. If not, White still has much to do, but he owns the cube, a big asset in this position, and stands a reasonable chance of equalizing the game.

It is tempting to go to W5 for it's perfectly safe. But it is safe *only* for this roll, and no matter what Red throws next time, the chances are that he will only become stronger.

This concept must be mastered, even if you often lose by employing it, for you will lose far more frequently by not being prepared to take such risks.

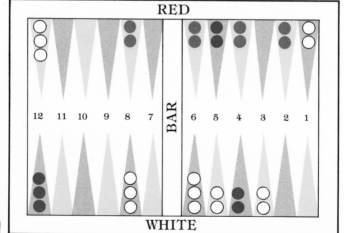

White to
play 6 – 2.

27

White is in command; he has excellent development and possession of both five points. Red has very little except his bar point, which is a questionable asset here. He also has a man on the rail and a blot on his four point. Realizing this, White should play the 4–3 boldly by starting his bar point from W11 and bringing another builder to W10, thus creating diversification to make W7 or W3 next time. The trap to avoid is the pusillanimous W11 to W8, covering. It looks nice but this is the time for White to be bold in án effort to lock Red in. He is strong in every aspect of the game and runs little risk with such wide-open play.

Too many positions in backgammon are not diagnosed thoroughly. People learn certain principles, such as "Make points where possible"; they fail to think any further and follow these rules out of context. Look for the specific priority during each move as the game progresses and the emphasis shifts from one area to another.

As a further basic example, let's say that your opponent runs with an opening 6–5 and that you reply with a 4–2, making W4. He then rolls another 6–5, and again runs. You now get a 3–1. It is only your second roll, and yet already you have to go against what you have been taught! Do *not* make your five point, but start his five point instead. Since both of his back men are temporarily safe, you must try to cover his outfield in an attempt to hit one of his men. Much of backgammon demands this ability to adjust and improvise.

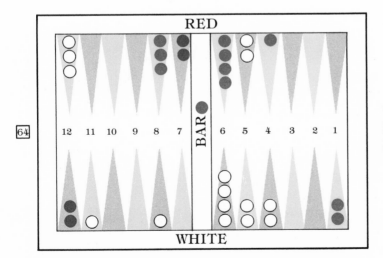

RED

64

12 11 10 9 8 7 BAR 6 5 4 3 2 1

WHITE

White to play 4–3. Red is on the bar.

28

This early position is simple but instructive because it illustrates two important aspects of the game. On White's previous roll he hit Red, who failed to enter. White thereupon doubled and Red accepted. In all money games this is a clear-cut take. If you are Red, up against a more experienced opponent, grab this double early in any tournament match. Your position is far from hopeless; you have W1 and cannot be blitzed, your timing is good and, most important, you own the cube and can create great leverage for yourself should the game turn in your favor. Don't be bluffed into a drop here just because you failed to enter. It is criminal to watch a tyro fold in such positions, because they present him with by far his best chance to score an upset. Later on, however — say 17 – 17 in a 21-point match — it becomes a more difficult take. If he is White, the tyro should definitely double, and even though the gammon threat is present, Red should take. Certainly the expert will double if White and correctly drop if Red because he doesn't dare expose himself to losing a gammon here.

But how should this 3 – 2 be handled? There is nothing difficult about it, but White must not be too conservative. The builder created by playing the three to W5 is important, and the two should be played from R7 to R9. If you thought of saving that blot on R7 by going all the way to W12, you have a lot to learn. Here is an opportunity to take a small voluntary risk to improve your already strong position. There are many early situations requiring similar tactics, and you must try always to be aware of them.

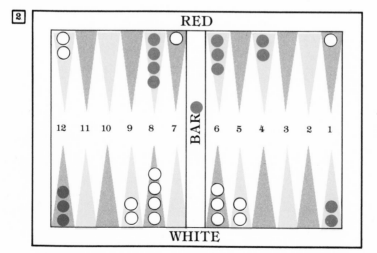

White to
play 3 – 2.
Red is on
the bar.

29

Often in backgammon — and in most other games as well — people tend to panic and thus make matters worse when disaster looms. In a reverse way that's what could occur in this problem; if White hit on R7, it would be tantamount to panicking because of excessive greed. He should keep his wits about him and realize that all his resources should be directed toward hitting Red's blot on W1. He can't do so — or certainly shouldn't — on this roll, but he must increase his chances as much as possible for his next shot in case Red fails to roll a one now. If he brings a man to W8 he will be able to hit with a 5 − 2 or 4 − 3, and will now be a 2 − 1 favorite to land on W1, the only point he cares about at this moment. The blot on R7 can wait; White can pick it up at his leisure later if he so wishes.

The fact is that if White manages to close out Red completely, he would do well to ignore the blot on R7. With three men on the bar and six others that Red must bring home, White has all but guaranteed himself a gammon if not hit. By picking up this fourth man it may allow Red just enough time to remain on the bar so that ultimately he gets a shot.

This problem looks deceptively simple, but two vital tactics are employed which are often overlooked. Be sure of your priorities when picking up blots, and don't be in a hurry to hit men you don't need, for they may haunt you later on.

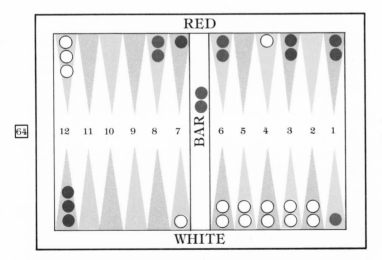

RED

64

12 11 10 9 8 7 BAR 6 5 4 3 2 1

WHITE

White to play 3 − 2.

30

This is an extremely complicated back-game position. Despite its appearances, the game is about even, and since he is playing a back game, White must try to prepare for all eventualities. What is his objective? First he must realize that though holding the one, two and three points in Red's board has been advantageous up to now, it could soon be a liability. Since the two most desirable to hold are your opponent's two and three points, this is an excellent time to break R1. It not only keeps R2 and R3 intact, but will release a man when White next rolls a six. More important, this assures White that Red must move and advance his front block. Consider, for example, how Red would have to play double 5's. He could play only three of them, two of them from R6 to R1, hardly what Red wants. If R1 were not broken, Red could play only one five and would maintain his formidable block. The four should be played from R12 to W9, so that Red (unless he rolls 6–1) will have to hit somewhere if he wants to free his back man.

Back games are difficult and dangerous. When you get into one, always try to position your men so that you can handle disaster shots (as double 6's would be for White here if he hadn't moved to R3). Conversely always be aware of possible horror shots for your opponent, and move your men so that he will be forced to play them and thus perhaps destroy an otherwise sound position.

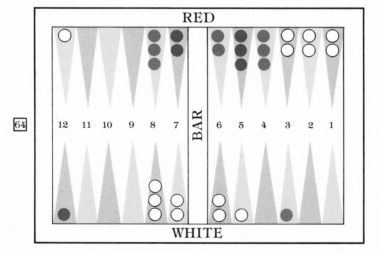

White to
play 4–2.

12 11 10 9 8 7 BAR 6 5 4 3 2 1

RED

WHITE

64

31

Here is an interesting early position that can be played in either of two ways. White can make his four point, hitting Red's blot, or he can make his bar and his opponent's five point. Which is better? It is a difficult choice and depends on other factors. Is it a money game where White is a novice pitted against an expert? If so, it would behoove White to refrain from hitting. He should secure R5 and W7, and then, with his defense coordinated, he can subsequently attack boldly. If the expert was White, however, I believe that pointing on W4 is best.

These tactics would also hold true in most tournament situations — with one exception: if the score was tied two points away from victory for either player, making W4 should be chosen regardless of the players' strengths. White has a small chance for a gammon this way, and at that score he should take it.

When expert is playing expert, I think making the bar and R5 is the best choice. The more you play, the more you will realize the value of your opponent's five point. Too often I've had the chance to make it early at the expense of other reasonable alternatives, have been talked out of it and wound up paying. Throughout this book you have been told over and over about the strength of this point. So even if you are given alternative choices in a specific case like the above, you will never be far wrong if you decide to make R5 willy-nilly.

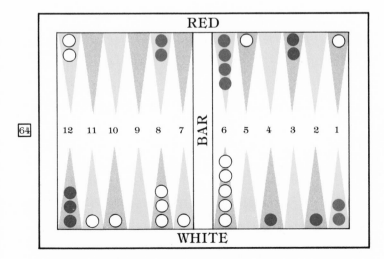

RED

64   12   11   10   9   8   7   BAR   6   5   4   3   2   1

WHITE

White to play 4 – 3.

$\mathcal{32}$ Except for double 4's, there could hardly be a better shot for White. After entering both men he has several options. He could: (A) make R4 or R3; (B) hit on W9; (C) hit inside his board from W8 to W4. All of these are reasonable, but one is by far the strongest. Of all the points on the board which is the most critical at this moment? W4, of course, and this is where White should direct all his attention. Since he has two points in Red's board, he has a fine defense and can afford to play wide-open, going into a massive back game if necessary. He should hit on W4 from W8, putting another of Red's men on the bar. If Red fails to roll a four or double 2's, White will be a prohibitive favorite to cover W4 on his next turn.

It is important to note how superior this play is to hitting Red's man on W9 from R12. In fact, even if White *knew* that Red was going to roll a four, he should still choose the suggested play, because if not hit, Red would establish this point and thereby equalize the game. Safety is not important here; W4 is, and White must go for it.

When there are options, as in this case, it is a vital skill to differentiate when to hit inside and when outside your board. Sometimes your position demands exactly the opposite of what you should do here. If you feel that being hit twice in a blot-hitting contest would be a disaster, then it is probably best for you to hit outside. But here, even if Red rolls double fours, you are not destroyed by being hit twice; thanks to your strong position and balance, your risk is minimal. This roll offers a great opportunity to put yourself in command.

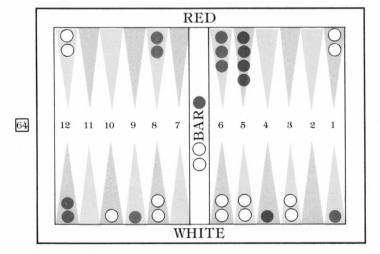

White to play 2 – 2. He has two men on the bar, and Red has one

33 This is a complicated position that stresses the importance of timing. It is obvious that White rolled double 5's earlier; as a result, his board is weak and he must be aware that he is not ready to abandon R7 in order to hit. A good concept to keep in mind is the following: if I elect to pick up a blot and my opponent fails to reenter but my overall position has not appreciably improved, it was probably an error to hit. Here is a perfect example. If White sacrifices R7 in order to hit and Red stays out, Red still has a strong game because of his superior timing and that valuable point on W7.

The correct handling of this 2 – 2 is not easy. After you have rejected hitting, do not fall into the trap of making W11 and starting W4. It is perfectly safe and looks nice, but it is wrong. You would now be stripped everywhere, with no spare men, and would have to pray for a 5 – 5 or 4 – 4 to keep you afloat. The best play is to make W4 and save the blot on R10, leaving a man open on W8 vulnerable to a one. You will then have a formidable four-point board and four men on your midpoint, all very much in play. Furthermore, if Red gets a one and elects to hit, his defense is gone, and should you enter and hit back, you would be in command if he stayed out, because he would no longer hold W7. In addition, if White is hit with a one and fails to enter, he is still far from beaten because he has R7.

In most games it is difficult to refrain from hitting whenever possible, but you must look ahead and in certain critical instances realize that different tactics are mandatory.

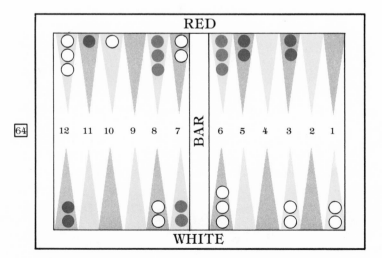

White to
play 2 – 2.

34   This is as pretty a problem as you could find, and it occurred in a low-stake, head-to-head game. Not surprisingly, White was elated with his 5 – 2 and quickly played the two to R4 and made W4 with the five. I was kibitzing, and when I asked if I could jot down the position, I was allowed time to do so.

Nobody can really fault White's choice, but on analysis is it correct? I don't think so. Red has that priceless extra man to play from R12, so unless White gets a direct five on his next roll he will have to break his newly formed five-point block. Once that goes, White's timing will be destroyed, so his best bet here is to go all the way from R2 to R9. This not only duplicates ones and threes — that is, W2 and W4, to either of which Red would like to advance — but also releases a vital man; should Red not get a one or a three, White will be in command. Moreover, even if Red gets a 5 – 3, hitting twice, White still will have an excellent back game.

This is not an easy problem, for the urge to make W4 and secure that five-point block is very strong. But White is not quite ready to block Red yet; he must first get his back men out or make Red break his front position. By moving to R9, White keeps his game in balance, being ready for all possible shots by the opposition.

Timing, which is the essence of a large percentage of backgammon tactics, is perhaps illustrated here more dramatically than in any other problem in this book.

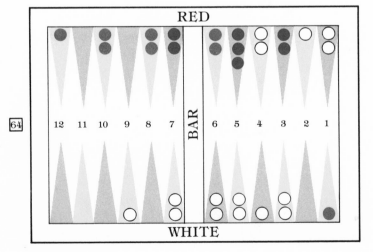

RED

64   12   11   10   9   8   7   BAR   6   5   4   3   2   1

WHITE

White to
play 5 – 2.

35

White has R2 and R3, the best two points for a back game, but his timing is not good and his having made W2 is a liability. Still, his position is flexible, and he can shift into a front or back game as a result of this move.

White should hit the blot on W3 with a man from W6, and leave men open on W3 and W4. Many players will regard this as foolhardy, but the point is that if Red reenters, White needs the delay and therefore wants to be hit. On the other hand, there is a chance (3–1 against) that Red will stay on the bar; if this occurs, White may be able to cover his inner blots on W3 and W4, hit Red again on W10 and have time to extricate his back men with sixes, fives and fours. Hence, at this moment White is not irrevocably committed to either plan; his decision will be made after Red's next roll.

To try to keep all options open as long as possible is an important part of backgammon. The reason White can do so here is that his escape routes are open. For example, if Red's men were on R7 instead of W12, thus forming a solid five-point block, White would have to commit himself totally to a back game and should play to force Red to hit him. Therefore he would hit Red from W5 with the two and break W2, starting W1, with the one. Then Red would have to hit somewhere, just what White wants, unless he rolled double 6's. Ideally, in this position White would hope that Red rolled a 6–1, forcing him to hit on W1, and if Red should later opt for more blots, White would welcome their being recirculated.

Under no circumstances should White hit the blot on W10 with this 2–1. However, if Red stays on the bar, White could then direct his attention to this blot.

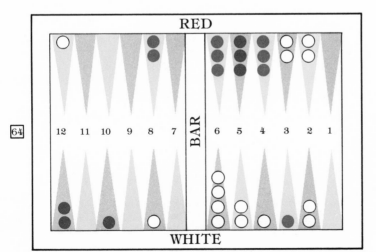

White to
play 2–1.

36

Red has been doubled and is on the ropes, so White must endeavor to keep him there. The choice is: (A) cover W3; (B) hit Red on W2 and bring a man down to W11, creating another builder in White's outer board.

This is an enjoyable problem because with either play White figures to win; it is not a crucial life-and-death decision. But it is important to follow a policy of aggressiveness in such positions. Red has no offense or defense, whereas White has fine development plus the anchor on R4 just in case. Therefore he should attack with every resource to keep Red reeling. By all means, hit on W2 instead of covering W3.

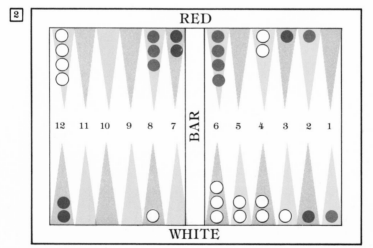

White
to play 2 – 1.

37

This 6 – 4 is an excellent shot for White. He is forced to enter on R4, but has a choice of sixes. It would be most natural to hit on R7, releasing a man from R1 and preventing Red from making R7 – both worthwhile objectives – and many would do so. But White's timing is excellent, and what he wants is to make Red play; he doesn't wish to slow him up now by hitting him. Thinking the problem through, he should realize that on balance hitting would delay Red's progress and be beneficial to him. Therefore he should start his own bar point with the six, leaving a three shot and not minding being hit. In any case, Red will have to move and White's board figures to be improved for a probable later shot, or even double shot.

To make the suggested move may seem perverse, but it is the result of logical reasoning. So much of backgammon is like this: apparently complicated plays are the result of a series of simple concepts.

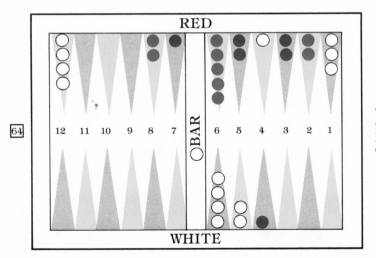

White
to play 6 – 4.
He is
on the bar.

38

This problem might be described as the opposite of a dilemma, because whatever choice is made, it is a powerful shot for White. Try to train yourself in positions such as this to play your forced or obvious sixes immediately. Surely it is correct to make W5, so do this first. Now you have your option of starting one bar and making the other, a pleasant if difficult decision. So start both bars. Now you have played three sixes and have only one left, so you can devote your complete attention to it. Too many people try to decide at once what they will do with all four, as if they had to move them simultaneously, but it makes much more sense to approach the problem methodically.

Whichever fourth six you choose cannot be criticized; it is really a matter of style. Is it worth leaving thirty shots which hit on R7 to secure W7 and a five-point block? Or would it be better to make R7, leaving just a six for a total of only fifteen shots? This is another case where there is no clear-cut right or wrong answer. My own preference, admittedly slight, would be to make R7, for it creates a defense and gives White's game more balance. White would have a very strong frontal position if he made W7, but he would be abandoning all his defense by this move. If he thinks it's worth it he should play this way, but he should remember that the concept of defense is not negative thinking. Would you call the role of pitchers in baseball, goalies in hockey or linebackers in football negative positions? Hardly—each is a positive defensive force which wins at least as many games as the so-called offense. Pick whichever play you deem correct here, but always be aware of the indispensability of a sound defense, whether in backgammon or any other game.

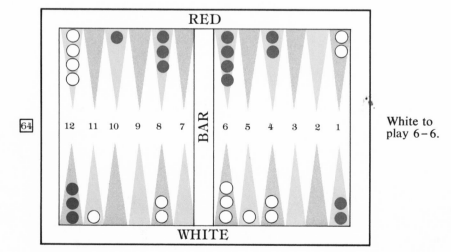

White to play 6–6.

39

White must realize that Red, who has W5 and whose timing is superior, is much better placed than he. These conditions dictate that White take positive action. He could save the man on R11, but that would be too passive. He could also make W4, strengthening his board, but then he would be stripped almost everywhere. What he must now do is activate his back men at all costs, but how? He could bring them both up from R1, but then would run a risk of being hit twice. He has to worry about his blot on W11 as well and he could be picked up with four separate numbers: fives, threes, twos and ones. Instead, he has a constructive and less dangerous move. He should start R3 by splitting from R1, and move the four to W10. By doing this he is vulnerable only to fives and threes; of course 5 – 5 or 3 – 3 would finish him (that is, he couldn't take a double); yet since he must attack with very little ammunition, this way seems strongest. If White survives, he may make an advanced anchor in Red's board, and his position will then be almost equal to his opponent's.

Again, this problem is not difficult, but it demonstrates that there often comes a critical time early in the game when definite action is mandatory. White cannot afford to sit back and wait; he must make something happen *now*.

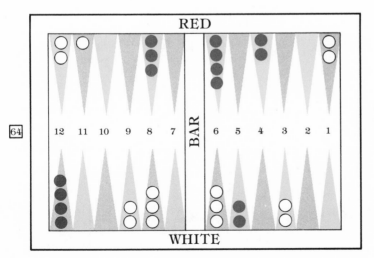

RED

64

12 11 10 9 8 7 BAR 6 5 4 3 2 1

WHITE

White to
play 4 – 2.

40

White should make W4 instead of covering W9 and adding to W8. What Red wants is to secure W7, so if he hits White with a one he abandons this vital point. In addition, by getting W4, White not only creates a strong four-point board but also makes holding his two point less awkward. Without securing W4 or W3, his men on W2 are too isolated. It is natural to bring two men down safely from R12, but Red has no board, and to do so would not be using the roll to best advantage.

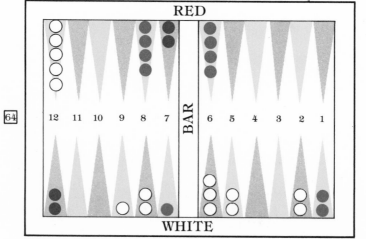

White to play 5–4.

41 There is a natural aversion to leaving two blots, no matter what the situation. But there are times when this predilection should be ignored. White should make W4 here, leaving his men exposed on the ten and eleven points. By doing so, he locks in Red's men on W2 except for fives; moreover, even if White is hit, Red's board is not yet formidable. Besides, Red will probably have to break a valuable defensive point, W7, if he chooses to hit, and thus will be vulnerable to being primed if White can subsequently make W7. White's timing may actually be improved if hit. A play like this may look foolhardy, but when analyzed it has to be correct in the long run.

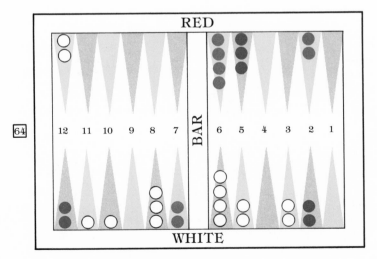

64

RED

12 11 10 9 8 7 BAR 6 5 4 3 2 1

WHITE

White to
play 4–2.

42

It is tempting to make W11 with this 3 – 2, and many would do so. But Red's board is too strong to risk another man back; in addition, White would be conceding control of Red's outfield too early. Sometimes the unimaginative play is best. White should save the blot on R11 by moving to W9 and keep R12 as a landing place for his back man. Once again the four-point block against Red's anchor on W5 looks strong, but Red is in no hurry to break, preferring to hold that vital point while attempting to build up a block of his own on R7 and R8.

Incidentally, assume that White plays the 3 – 2 as suggested above and Red now throws a 6 – 2. Because of his powerful board Red should boldly start R7 and split to R4. Due to the position, his tactics are directly the opposite of White's. If White does not hit either blot (he is 19 – 17 not to) Red becomes a pronounced favorite and should double, partly because of his excellent gammon chances. In many tournament situations White would have to drop, but in a money game anyone who takes such a double cannot be faulted.

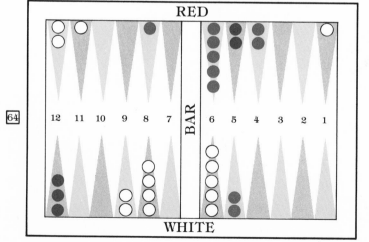

White to
play 3 – 2.

43

In all money games the answer is "Definitely not." White's position looks formidable, but this is something of a mirage. First of all Red's position on W8 is very strong, and White's having lost control of his outfield is a weakness. A further deterrent to doubling is that Red has no additional men open. To give up the cube here would be an error, for it would allow your opponent too much leverage.

On the other hand, in a tournament when a gammon is vital, White might double. If, for example, the score was 11 – 11 in a fifteen-point match, White might risk it. But even here – and particularly if the score was 13 – 11 either for or against him – Red should accept. Of course there is danger in taking, for 6 – 6 or 3 – 3 could cost Red a gammon, but in practically every game one side or the other could lose a gammon if his opponent rolls the perfect shot.

Too many playable positions are dropped when the opponent doubles. This applies to all standards of play, even to the experts. The cube is by far the most misunderstood and mishandled aspect of the game. Virtually no one yet has a true grasp of its significance. This is not surprising because it came into use relatively recently.

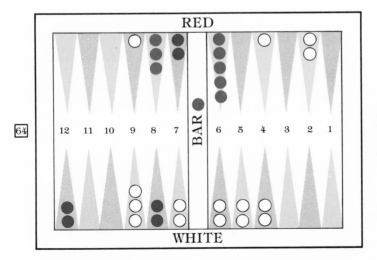

Red is on the bar. White to roll. Should he double?

44 Red is already far ahead in the race, and the natural inclination would be for White to hit on R4 to slow down his opponent. But Red's timing is bad; he has lost control of the outfield, so that his line of communications between his two back men and the rest of his forces has been broken by his having abandoned the midpoint. Here is still another example of how unimportant the race is early in the game. Position is what counts, and White has it. He should ignore the blot on R4 and make W5. If Red replies with any big number he is all but lost, and if he should hit the blot that White has left on W8 he cannot protect R4 as well. If Red doesn't hit he may make R4, but White will be in a strong position with those men on R12 poised to add other points to those White already has on W7, W6 and W5. It would be a mistake for W1 to be trapped into hitting on R4; such a move would vastly improve Red's chances of making a forward point on White's board which he needs desperately to survive.

Suppose, however, that Red's blot were on R5. Then, of course, White should use this roll to hit him; he cannot afford to let Red have this point by default.

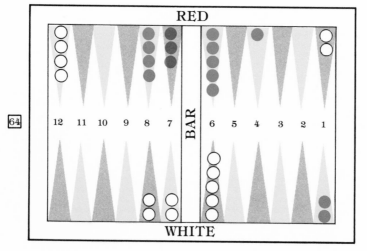

64

White to
play 3 – 1.

45

Red is in a great position to make either his five point or his bar. White would like to hit him somewhere to thwart either of these plays, but with this roll he cannot do so. To come in on R2 and move a man down to W8 is being too easy on Red, and allows him many options. To enter on R5 and stay there is foolhardy; it is too dangerous with all the ammunition trained on that point. So what should White do? The answer is simply to start R7. This may seem martyrlike, but if you look a little deeper you see that even if Red points on White on R7, he cannot build up his board unless he rolls 1–1. Had White stayed on R5 and Red had made that point, White's problems would be much greater. Red has almost succeeded in getting his forces safely home, and White must create a diversion to offset this. Even though he seems to be leading with his chin, this is his best attacking play; he must not be passive here.

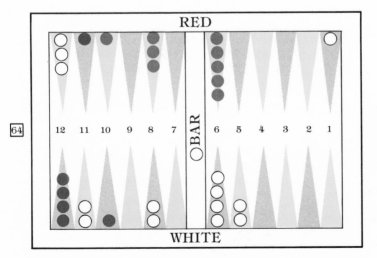

White to play 5 – 2 from the bar.

46

Here is a position about which many players will disagree. White must enter on R5, and now has to decide on his two. Either (A) he comes out to R7, or (B) he hits on W7. White may think that hitting is best, but he should consider a few things first. He has been doubled, and now is in danger of being gammoned if he loses two men. (B) risks this; fourteen return shots hit somewhere, and if White doesn't immediately roll a five he will be in bad shape. If he elects (A) he leaves sixteen shots, two more than if he hit on W7, but now only one man is vulnerable. R5 is open, and it may be a while before Red closes it. Also, there are eight numbers— 1–1, 2–1, 3–1, 2–2, and 3–4—where Red will have to give White a direct return shot if White selects (A).

What it amounts to is this: is it worth risking a gammon to choose (B) and be two shots better off? Of course (A) may lose a gammon too, and since it is less aggressive it will make it more difficult for White to win than (B) would be—assuming, of course, that White is not hit no matter which he chooses.

Every so often it is instructive to include a problem for which there is no definite right or wrong. Here is an example. When all the angles have been considered, both (A) and (B) have merit. If, for instance, White is ahead 13–11 in a fifteen-point match, he would be wise to limit his liability and select (A). If a gammon was irrelevant, however, as they sometimes are—14–14, for instance—it would be a mistake not to choose (B), since it offers White the best chance not to be hit.

Everything being equal, in tournaments and in all money games, I would opt to follow the old principle "When in doubt hit." If hit back, I'd simply pray hard for a five—a welcome return shot no matter which play is selected.

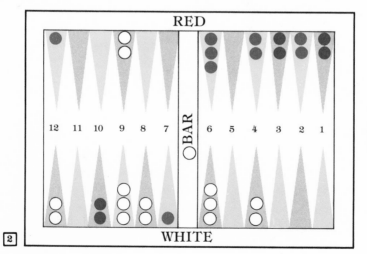

White to play 5–2 from the bar.

47 White's position is awkward. Earlier he rolled a 5–5 and tried unsuccessfully for a blitz by hitting and making W1. Now he will be plagued by that miserable point for the rest of the game. The six covers nicely from R9 to W10; there is hardly any other choice, and now White must decide on the four. He has escaped Red's board with his back men and is well ahead in the race, but much as he would like to play safe and go to W2 from W6, he must resist the temptation. He does not relish being sent back because Red's board has a strong potential; nevertheless, his best play is to start W9 and risk being hit with a five. He already has four men out of play (on W3 and W1), and if he moves still another off W6, he will be stripped on three points, W6, W8 and W10. Even if Red misses him on W9, White will still have problems, but they would be far worse if he went to W2 now.

Temporary safety is an illusion in backgammon. Some players can never be convinced that voluntary risks have to be taken to guard against later disaster. There was a marvelous old gentleman I used to play with who couldn't understand the need for these apparently suicidal plays. His philosophy always was, "Why look for trouble where there ain't none?" His error was in assuming that just because trouble wasn't in immediate evidence it would never crop up — sophistry of the first order.

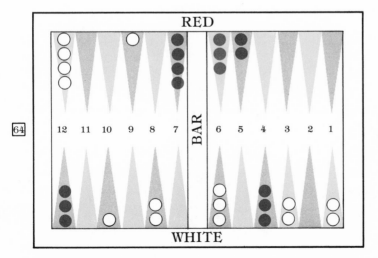

64

RED

12 11 10 9 8 7 BAR 6 5 4 3 2 1

WHITE

White to play 6–4.

48 With this roll Red has the best of the situation for the moment; White must take some positive action. Red is about to close R5, which White can't prevent, so he has to find a move which will make his position more equal. Hence he starts by rejecting the safe and purposeless move of R12 to W8. He should consider starting W10 and W4, leaving two blots but duplicating threes; he could also start W11 and put a builder on W5, which would leave two blots in his outer board. But they would not be in great danger because if Red should manage to hit either, he could not cover R5. So often this is the case; train yourself to be aware of such a position when it arises, and it will enable you to make the correct move instead of playing safe when there is no need to. White could also activate his back men by starting R3 and bringing the three down to W10. Though White's board is good enough to deter Red from getting too rambunctious, breaking R1 here is too dangerous. Either of the other two plays is worth making; they both have merit and it's a tossup which is better. I myself would start W4 and W10, but can find no fault with starting W11 and adding a builder on W5. Either of these is far superior to the other choices.

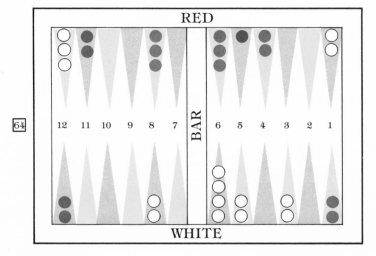

RED

64

12   11   10   9   8   7   BAR   6   5   4   3   2   1

WHITE

White to play 3–2.

49 White had a blitz going and had to slot a man on W5 to pick up a third Red man. Red replied with double 5's, hitting on W5 and W10. Now White has rolled 2 – 2; he must enter on R2 and decide where to play the other two 2's.

Surprisingly, the blots on W7 and W9 are not really vulnerable because Red should keep that anchor on W5, which is his only strength. The blot on R11 can't move, and to advance its companion on R10 to W11 doesn't accomplish anything. What is left? By far the most useful way to play the rest of the shot is to make R4. This seems a terrible price to pay for a forward anchor; the natural impulse is to make W7 and look around for a fourth two. But this is a time to improvise and make an unorthodox move. The four blots—five if you count the man on R1—are a liability, but for the moment White can't concern himself with them. He has just been struck an almost lethal blow (the double 5's) and has to keep his wits about him and look to his defenses. This 2 – 2 is a lifesaver, enabling him to put both men back in play and secure a forward anchor as well. There isn't time for a back game; White is fighting to survive and badly needs a defense.

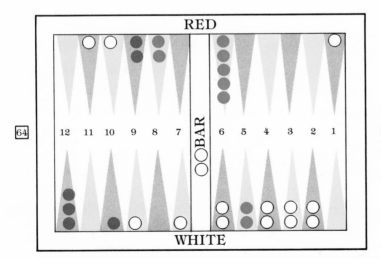

White to play 2 – 2. He has two men on the bar.

50

In practically all money games, whether head-to-head or chouette, White should definitely not double here. Red doesn't have the best back game with those five and two points, but his timing is reasonable and White is awkwardly situated to play sixes. Some people would look at this position and be bewildered by the question below. Of course White shouldn't double, they would say; Red's board is good, and already there are disaster shots possible, such as 6−5 or 6−2. But though we agree completely with retaining the cube in money games, the position is far more complicated in a tournament, and is worth looking into.

One of the great weapons the inexperienced player could have over the expert is learning to handle the cube properly in leverage situations. This moment is admittedly dangerous, for one bad roll could destroy White. But assume that White, a comparative novice, is pitted against a champion in a fifteen-point tournament match, and that the score is 11 all; how do you think the expert would like to be doubled here? If another expert were across the table, he might take his chances, but is he going to risk being gammoned by a tyro here? My guess is that he would drop, unhappy that he was not allowed to play on with the cube at one. But he would be dead right in doing so; he doesn't want the whole match riding on one game, and correctly relies on his expertise to see him through to ultimate victory.

Now let's reverse the players: White is the expert and Red the tyro. If White doubles here, instead of dropping, Red should grab the cube quickly before his opponent changes his mind. Furthermore, he should redouble *immediately*, no matter what White's next roll is. Thus, the whole match will hinge on this game—correct tactics for Red. White's only reason for doubling in the first place would be that he had misjudged Red and

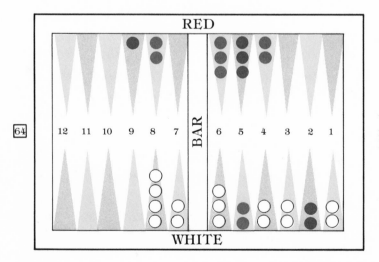

White to roll. Should he double?

thought he would drop. If there is a remote chance of Red taking, White should be stripped of his expert rating for doubling.

The subtle advantages of the doubler should be pored over by all aspiring players. It is pathetic to watch matches in which the expert psychs out his inexperienced opponent, when the latter has such a weapon at hand if only he realized it, and which the expert cannot use.

51

This is a beautiful shot for White, and he must not fall into the trap of hitting on W10. To make W5 here is by far his strongest play. Many players have an incurable aversion to leaving a double shot, but leave it White should. By holding R7, he has a fine defense, and also threes and ones are duplicated; that is, Red needs these numbers to cover R5 as well as hit.

Even if Red had a better board, White should make his five point. This is not a difficult decision, but it is important to conquer such hang-ups as leaving a double shot. "When in doubt, hit" is a winning philosophy, but when this position is analyzed, there is no doubt that W5 is best.

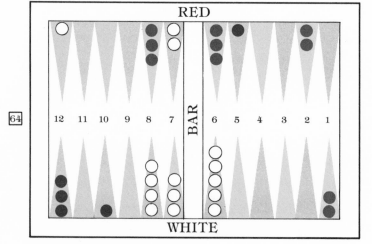

White to
play 3 – 2.

52

It is early, but Red is off to a fast start and has already doubled. The two best choices are: (A) enter on R1 and hit on W4; (B) enter on R4 and move to R10. Under no circumstances should White move the man on R1. Throughout your backgammon life you will be advised to attack when cornered to create a diversion and keep your opponent busy; indeed, there are many such recommendations in this book. Therefore it is instructive to run across a position that looks as if it demands action but in reality doesn't. Though it is risky — what isn't? — in this position (B) is better; enter on R4 and move to R10. Admittedly, White is vulnerable, but only fours, threes and a double two can hurt him. Moreover, he lacks builders in his own board. To select (A) and bury two men back on R1 is much safer for the moment, but entirely too cautious; in effect White is virtually abdicating the game. This recommended play might be called a passive attack. What White is trying for is R4, and he has an excellent chance to make it if not hit, or if Red hits only the outside man on R10.

To enter on R1 and hit on W4 would perhaps be considered too bold by many players, but (B) is in many ways bolder. It courts destruction, but everything considered, it gives White his best chance to develop a playable position to offset Red's strength.

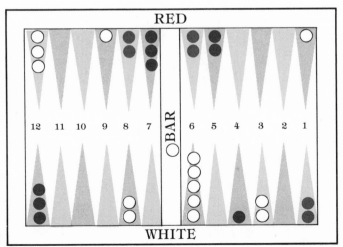

White to
play 4 – 1.
He is
on the bar.

53

This is an excellent position because it almost demands that White start W7; there is little else he can do with the six. Even the most chicken-hearted would rebel at playing W11 to W5, and making W2 this early goes against anyone's grain. Starting the bar in these situations isn't done often enough. But it is important to have some kind of an anchor in your opponent's board, so that if he misses you on W7, he can't attack you elsewhere.

The game is at a critical stage, and Red wants R5 as much as White wants W7. But if Red is to make R5, he can't also hit on W7 (except with 3 – 3), so White must take this risk. Further, he must continue to be bold by starting W10 with the three; don't justify playing W11 to W8 by telling yourself that you've been daring enough in leaving a six shot. Of course White doesn't want to be hit twice, which he will be if Red rolls 6 – 3 or 6 – 4 (with 3 – 3 he would make R5), but the potential of those builders in White's outer board are worth the gamble.

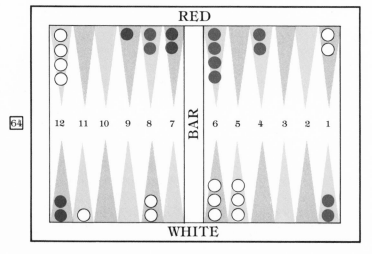

White to play 6 – 3.

54

White is too far ahead of himself, and this 6 – 5 only adds to his woes. He has been doubled and is in bad shape. What can he do here? Red has a formidable front position, with fine potential for improvement. But a blessing for White is that so far Red's inner board contains only two points. White can't afford to have Red make any more, so, awkward though it is, White's best chance is to make the unnatural play of pointing on W1. There are a score of possibilities he would prefer — covering W4, for one — but since he has no decent alternative he may as well hit and secure a three-point board. If Red should fail to enter (he is a 3 – 1 favorite to come in), White will have gained a valuable tempo, may cover W4 and could extricate himself from a difficult predicament. At least by making W1, he is likely to restrict Red from improving his board.

This position also emphasizes the value of owning the cube. If Red had access to it and decided to double here, after this 6 – 5, White would be hard pressed to accept. But since White is not vulnerable, having already been doubled, at least he can make any play he wants and not be forced out. A position such as this one enhances my conviction that doubles should be accepted if at all playable, especially when there is equity in owning the cube.

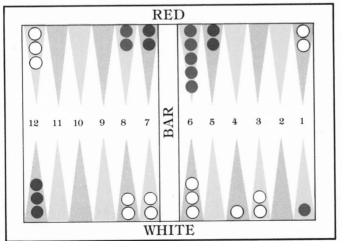

White to
play 6 – 5.

55 White has doubled early, but his position is strong and this 2 – 2 makes it even more so. He has Red on the defensive and should do everything possible not to let him regain his balance. The first two — making W4 — are automatic, but he must be careful of how he plays his other twos. It would be easy and natural to make W8 and then start W11, and too many would do so. What they haven't thought through is that because R5 is open, no matter how many blots are left in White's outer board, none of them can be hit with impunity, regardless of Red's roll! In other words, Red can't both hit and cover. Therefore White should start W9, spreading three blots, all builders for the bar along with the men on R12. He dares Red to hit any of these — and look at Red's position if he chooses to do so! He will have four blots open around the board and no defense whatsoever.

Similar opportunities occur frequently, and players should train themselves to spot them when they arise. Compare the difference in potential for White between the two moves — and consider also that the extra risk is negligible.

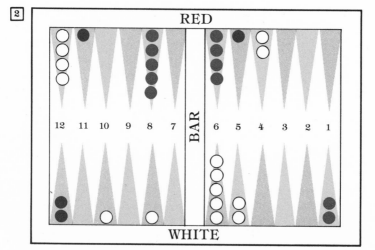

White to
play 2 – 2.

56

Both sides have solid defensive anchors, but Red's timing is better, so White must not help him by hitting here. It would accomplish little to send another man back with no board to contain him. White should cover W4 and bring his outside man to W10. He welcomes being hit because this will enable him to enter R's board and play from there without breaking R4. The timing for both sides is critical.

An interesting decision for Red would arise if he next rolled a 5 – 1. It would be difficult to resist the obvious: hitting on W10 and then covering his man on W11. But this would be wrong because Red would now be stripped everywhere. It is a moot decision whether he should hit at all and merely play to R8 instead; if he does elect to hit, he should leave a blot on W10 and move the man on W11 to W12. This is superior to securing W11 because Red doesn't mind being hit, and also now has an extra man to play from W12.

This is yet another example of the aesthetic play – hitting and covering W11 – being incorrect. Positions like either White's or Red's here demand a sort of sixth sense. If I were Red and rolled a 5 – 1, my own preference would be to ignore the blot on W10, and play to R8. White might then make W10, creating a four-point block, but he would lose control of his outfield in doing so. Further, unless he rolls a double six, five or three, he is going to have trouble releasing his men on R4.

This started out as a problem for White, but has slowly turned into one for Red. However, that's a major purpose of this game: to try to create problems for your opponent.

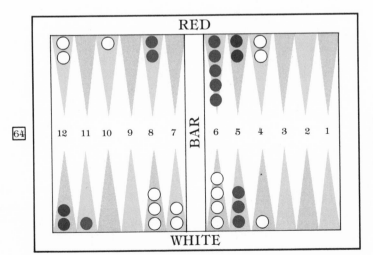

White to play 5 – 4.

57

White is ahead in the race, but he is going to have timing problems soon and Red has a better position. White would like to make W3, but then where would he play his four? There doesn't seem to be any alternative to moving from W9 to W2, leaving two blots in his board. Still, look at White's position if he makes this play. His outfield is stripped, and the three men marooned on R7 are badly placed. Therefore White should look hard for a better way to handle this 4–3. Though it is brave and could result in disaster—like almost any risky move—much the best play would be to move from R7 to W11, leaving a four and a six shot. To hit, Red would have to break W5, and White would have four places to enter, besides owning R7 as a defense. It is a mirage to overestimate Red's strength in this position. White would not mind being hit because it would help his timing, and if not hit, he may make W9 next timé and have a four-point block to make Red's escape more difficult.

Though this play shows a grasp of strategy, it would be dismissed immediately by the majority of players because it looks foolhardy. So much of backgammon is like this, however, and you simply can't pigeonhole such positions; they demand singular, unusual treatment. If, instead, White opts for the safe and aimless W2 move, he will soon be reduced to praying for a 5–5 in order to survive. Such optimism is not realistic. Don't be a pessimist, but don't rely on miracles either; they don't occur often enough.

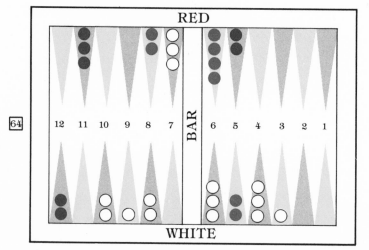

White to
play 4–3.

58

This is a fine early shot for White. He has many options, but should dismiss any that don't hit on W9. If left alone, Red is in position to make either his bar or his five point; in addition, White has his own five point, which restricts Red's reentry. But how to hit the man on R9? White could make W9 safely; he could hit with the two and come to R5; he could hit with the four and come to R3. Since Red will be on the rail, it is an excellent time for White to activate one of his back men in comparative safety. I believe that the best play is to hit with the four and split to R3. This split is usually dangerous, but notice how double fives are no threat here and that 3 – 3 is the only real horror shot. Another factor is that by playing this way it makes any six, except 6 – 3, bad for Red. Four blots are left around the board, but the risk is well calculated and, on balance, White will be much better situated if he takes this chance now, rather than lying back and perhaps getting his back men locked in.

Look for situations like this where you have protection when you elect to activate your back men; if you can avoid it, don't let your opponent have all his resources trained on one area.

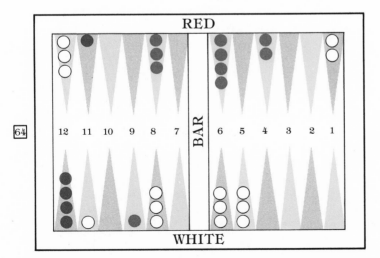

White to
play 4 – 2.

59

White would like to have another man on R4 so that he could release a six. But as is so often the case in a back game, his timing is suspect and he needs delay. What should he do? Probably best is to start both his bar and his three point. If Red wants to free his back man he will have to hit unless he rolls a 6–1, and this will give White a chance to make R3, securing three points in his opponent's board. From Red's point of view, the threat of W7 should not concern him. White is hardly in a position to play a blocking game yet; he would have a mammoth task in releasing his five men from Red's board. Still, most people in Red's position would hit with a six, glad to have escaped.

In the majority of back games, even where all men are in play, the advantage lies with the defender—that is, Red in this case. So many throws are bad for White, especially large numbers. If he can manage to keep his strong outside block until White has to advance his shaky board even further, Red will have much the best of it and pose a gammon threat.

Players are intrigued about learning how to play a back game, and it is exciting to bring one off, but be sure you also learn how to defend against this maneuver. You will find it much simpler and more financially rewarding, if less glamorous. When you are opposing a back game, don't be afraid of being hit yourself, because delay can help you too—a tactic which all too many players are unaware of.

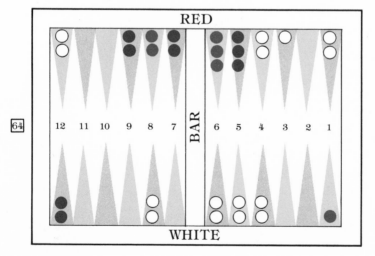

RED

12 11 10 9 8 7 BAR 6 5 4 3 2 1

64

WHITE

White to
play 5 – 1.

60 This is an enjoyable problem because there are so many ways to play it, and all of them have merit. White could use this great shot at least three times because he has many things to do with it. (A) he can come up to R4, hit on W7, and put a builder on W5; (B) he can hit on W7 and make W3; (C) he can make W7, hitting; (D) he can hit twice, leaving blots on W7 and W2; (E) he can point on W2, hitting.

(E) not only looks wrong, but is wrong, so it should be eliminated from further consideration. However, of the first four, which is best? It's difficult to choose, and impossible to state for certain. Coming to R4 is important, because if he is hit on W7, White will have a chance to make that important forward anchor. Making W7 and forming a four-point block has merit because the two blots left on R10 and R12 are partially duplicated, Red perhaps needing a one or a three to enter. Hitting twice would be great if Red failed to get a two and also rolled a five or a six, but this seems too remote.

I believe that (B) is best, even though it has the drawback of not duplicating either threes or fives, numbers to which White is vulnerable if Red enters. Making that extra point (W3), especially with Red on the bar, seems strongest. If he doesn't enter—he is a 3 – 1 favorite to do so—White has an excellent blitz opportunity, or at the least, a strong blocking game.

An incidental thought: though almost everyone would and should reject (E), look how much better it would be than (B) if Red now rolls a 2 – 2! Which proves that almost all backgammon moves, no matter how bad in theory, can be right if the dice land a certain way.

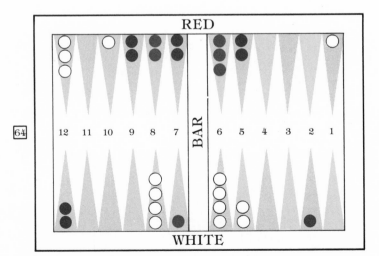

RED

64

12 11 10 9 8 7 BAR 6 5 4 3 2 1

WHITE

White to play 3 – 3.

61

This is presented as a dual problem in order to emphasize an important point. In each case White owns the cube. The positions look much alike and are similar, but different tactics should be used. Once again a paradox emerges. In (A) White already has a blot on R3, must enter on R5 and has no good four. His priority is to consolidate somewhere in Red's board. He has no board himself, is wide open with no defense, and yet the correct play is to hit on W4, exposing yet another man. By now this diversionary move is known to most players as a resourceful weapon. Since White has blots on both R5 and R3, and since his opponent will be on the bar after White hits him on W4, Red can't very well do everything; no matter what he rolls, on his next turn White will have a chance to make a defensive point. There is no safe play, but to come out to R9 or R7 instead of hitting would only lessen White's chances because he now would have only one place occupied in Red's board. By far the best play in this desperate spot is to be aggressive and hit on W4.

Now for (B). White enters with the three and has a two to play. Following the same concept, too many players would mistakenly hit on W4 here as well, but the situation is not the same at all. White has far less chance of establishing an anchor because only one man is in Red's board, which will be hit with a five. Furthermore, by hitting with the two, White will allow two more men to be vulnerable at a moment when his opponent's board is three times as good as his. This is the moment for White to retrench as best he can. He should save his man on W10, even though he has no development. Red has no inside builders and can hit only with a five. White hopes for some point-making shot next time if he can't save his blot on R3. His position is extremely awkward, but he must not compound his

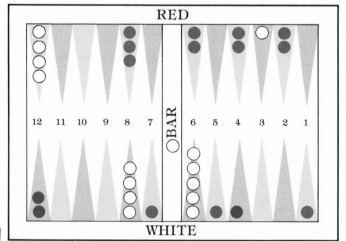

RED

12 11 10 9 8 7 BAR 6 5 4 3 2 1

WHITE

(A) White to play 5–4. He is on the bar.

troubles by making a play which has merit on other occasions but would be a disaster here.

If you can learn to distinguish between these two positions and then employ the correct tactics for each, you will have added valuable ammunition to your arsenal.

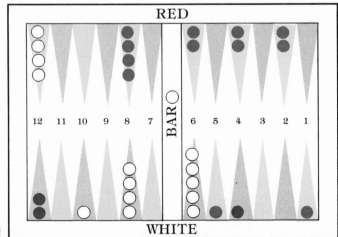

(B) White to play 3 – 2. He is on the bar.

62 White has a fine position, but has to be on his guard. He must not do the obvious, which is to make W8 with the two, securing a prime. Many would do this and play the four in from W7, feeling safe because Red can't release his back man. But what if Red now rolls a one and White fails to get his man out from R4? He might have to break his prime, and the game could turn around. The difficulty here is that White doesn't have a sure thing; therefore by far his best move is to hit on R1 with the builder on R7, sending a second man to the bar. Only a return of 1–1 or 2–2 really hurts, and he has a fine chance for a gammon if Red doesn't get either shot.

In this position it would be a major blunder to give Red a chance to consolidate. The suggested play looks daring, but paradoxically it is far less so than making a prime and ignoring Red's man on R1. Once again it is a matter of deciding what your overall purpose is. To make W8 looks tidy, but it is only one more example of playing in a vacuum. Be constantly on the alert for the obvious move — in this case making W8 — because so often it is a trap. The suggested play is White's best chance — not only for a gammon, but also for a single game. If Red establishes an anchor, he will be a threat till the end because he has good timing, owns the cube and can never be doubled out.

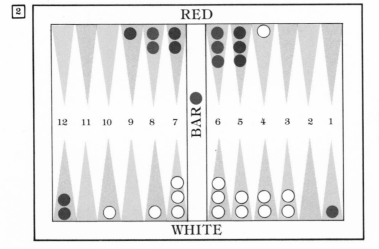

White to play 4–2. Red is on the bar.

63

Here is an example of the power of the cube. Red's board is top-heavy, and he has three men far back on W1. White has much more potential; all his men are in play, ready to make points. But there is one snag; he has a man on the bar facing a four-point board, perhaps even a five-point one after Red's roll. He will be a 5–4 favorite to enter if Red doesn't make R5 or R4. Red is a 7–5 underdog to make either, but if he succeeds, White will then become a 25–11 underdog to enter. It is tempting to accept; it is painful to give up in such a lopsided position, but the gammon threat is ominous. The man on W11 is vulnerable, but even without him, Red will probably win a gammon if he can close his board.

Hence the answer is that White should definitely not take. It is an astute double by Red; he is using the cube to ensure his win, not to double the stakes, for paradoxically he is very vulnerable. If White is allowed to play on, he could turn the situation around in one roll, so Red doubles, forcing White to drop.

There are desperadoes who would take this double but Red would welcome them; a take would give him a great chance to win four points, so he should be philosophical if he rolls double 5's or if White gets the miracle shot to extricate himself.

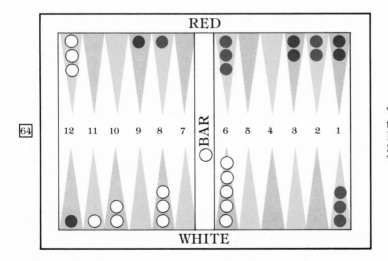

White is on the bar. Red doubles. Should White take?

64

White has been doubled and is in bad shape. His back men are about to be primed, and his two point is awkward. What should he do with this 6–1? He wants to stop Red from making R3, and the best way to do this is to hit if possible. He can hit on W1, but only at the expense of W7 or W8. Instinct should tell him that this play must be wrong, so the only move left is to bring the six to W7 and then decide on the one. It is difficult, but the conservative plays of bearing a man in to W6 or moving to W5, stripping W6, must be rejected. They do nothing for White. He has to start W4 bravely and pray. A lot can still happen: 5–5, 4–4 and 5–4 are all bad for Red, and if he does get a three or a one and hits, not only can he not improve his board (except for double 3's), but White will welcome the delay. To play safe and strip another point doesn't make sense in this situation. Here is one more example of taking a voluntary risk which isn't half as dangerous as it seems. Many a player in a worse position than this has survived.

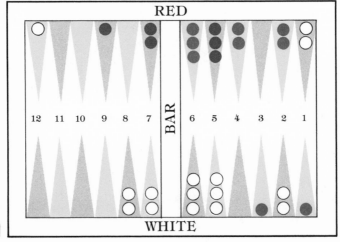

White to play 6–1.

2

65

White has doubled and is in a strong position. This is a simple problem, but White must be careful and not be lured into the obvious play of hitting twice on R5 and R11. Too many would jump at this chance to put two more men on the bar. Red already has one man up, and White should create another builder by starting W7 from R12 with the six. He can hit on R5 with the four, but the blot on R11 should be ignored for the present. Look at the avalanche awaiting Red if he enters on W4. Even if he fails to roll a five or a six and enters both men, White is almost sure to point on him somewhere; if not, he may hit Red twice.

Whenever positions like this arise, caution should be discarded in favor of an all-out blitz. A bonanza for Red would be 4–4, 3–3 or 1–1, and perhaps could turn the game around. But such possible miracles should not deter White. He must exploit his vastly superior position with every weapon at his disposal. To hit twice here, besides being greedy, would give Red a better opportunity to establish a point in White's board—just what White is trying to prevent. If Red did not have a man already on the bar, of course it would be correct to hit twice, but in this position the builder on W7 is too valuable to pass up.

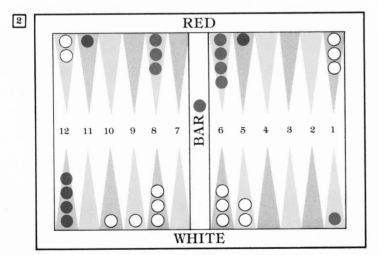

White to play 6–4. Red is on the bar.

66

White has a tempting play; he can make his two point, sending a second man to the bar and securing a four-point board. But this would be playing right into Red's hands, for it would allow him needed delay and let him retain his board if he failed to enter. Further, if he manages to enter with a three he will have another man to move. What White should do here is to arrange his men in an effort to make W8. If he moves his blot on R9 to W11 he will have three builders trained on this point. He shouldn't mind Red making W2, even though that will give him three points in White's board; if he can secure W8, in all likelihood his five-point block will force Red to break his board.

Red has a tenuous back game which White should be trying to break up rather than to assist. This position is an example of how much more desirable it is to defend against a back game than it is to play one. If White plays correctly, there are too many disaster rolls possible for Red. Remember to avoid back games unless there is no alternative, and learn to defend against them so that you will welcome your opponent trying to play one.

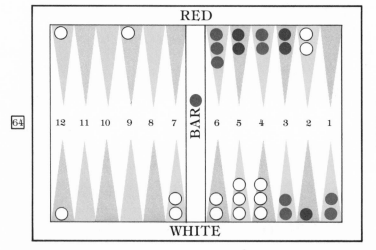

64

White to play 3 – 2. Red is on the bar.

67   Red is far ahead in a race, but White should resist hitting on W12 from R5 for three reasons. First, White is simply not yet ready to contain Red. His board is potentially strong but is not made up, and Red should have little trouble in escaping. Secondly, Red's timing is bad. He is stripped everywhere and soon will probably have to leave blots or put men out of play. He already has made R2 and R1, thus putting four valuable men out of action. Thirdly, Red owns W7. Without this point White might consider hitting and trying to block his opponent, but because of this escape valve he should be in no hurry to hit. Doing so would help Red's timing and perhaps allow him to maintain his tenuous position. In addition, the three and five points that White holds in Red's board are a bit advanced for a back game.

It is difficult not to hit, especially when you see that your opponent is far ahead and that you may not get another chance, but in this spot White must exercise patience. So many games are needlessly lost by hitting too early. Red is almost surely going to destroy himself soon if left alone, and White should wait quietly until this happens. By then he will be in better shape to hit and prevent Red's escape.

How, then, should White play this 4 – 4? Since he is so far behind in the race White should maintain both of his points in Red's board and concentrate on building up his own. Perhaps the best play would be to make W4 and put a builder in to W5. This leaves Red a three shot, but if hit White is in no great danger; moreover, if Red misses he will probably be in immediate trouble because he has only one spare man left (on R12) and soon will have to break some critical point. Meanwhile, with this roll, White has improved his board, and is poised to make his bar when Red leaves it, which he will have to do soon.

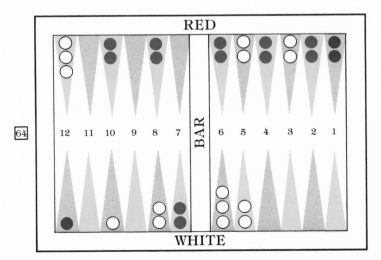

White to
play 4 – 4.

68

Obviously, this is a great shot for White, and of course he has to hit here or probably lose a gammon. He plays a man from R4 to R12, hitting, and now has two more fours to consider. Assuming that he leaves the blot on W8, how should he handle this? He wants desperately to make W5, but he must be careful because he still is vulnerable to losing a gammon if hit. Most people wouldn't think of putting a blot on W10 from R7 because double fives would hit. White is risking a 6 – 2 and 5 – 3 already, so why add a 5 – 5? But can you see why to do so must be correct? Basically, it is a matter of simple logic: whether or not White dares place that important builder on W10, Red is almost assured of a gammon if he rolls double 5's, even if he doesn't hit on the way! Therefore White's only concern should be those four shots he is exposed to by leaving his blot on W8. He could save this man, but in the long run such tactics are too conservative; he should stand his ground and take this 8 – 1 chance.

Once again the lesson here is to beware of the obvious. Beginners are taught to protect themselves from horror shots in critical situations, so too many of them would avoid starting W10 here because they don't realize that they have virtually nothing to lose and a lot to gain by leaving the extra shot.

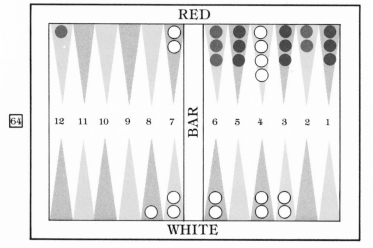

RED

64

12 11 10 9 8 7 BAR 6 5 4 3 2 1

WHITE

White to play 4 – 4.

69   I have to include this problem because it comes from perhaps the most important 'single game in which I've ever been involved. I've had a lot of fun with this 4–1. Whenever a group gathers and different positions are analyzed, I always produce this one and ask players which of two alternatives they would select: (A) making W4, leaving shots on R12 and W10; or (B) making W9, the outside point, and saving both blots. Usually the choice is about 50–50. I hardly endear myself by then announcing firmly to everyone that both plays are inept and categorically wrong!

The critical point which both sides want badly is R4. White can't make it with this roll, but that doesn't mean he has to give Red complete freedom to do so. He must create a diversion *now*, and the only way to do this is to hit Red on W1 from W6. By having to use one number to reenter, Red cannot exert all his attention on assaulting R4. By playing this way White is buying precious time which may let him secure R4 before Red does. White is in a bad way; he has to attack here with very little ammunition, but the alternative of retrenching and making either the irrelevant nine or four point is almost sure suicide.

In backgammon you should never give up till you are mathematically eliminated. After playing this game for only a short while, everyone becomes aware of what havoc the dice can cause from any position.

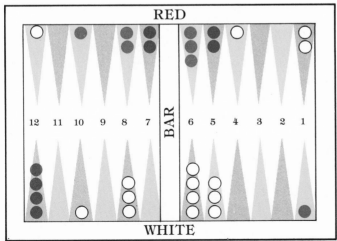

White to
play 4–1.

70 There will be a lot of arguments about this problem, for almost everyone would pounce on Red's blot on R7 and then make W1. The first part is correct, but even though Red has a four-point board buttoning up on W1 is wrong. Red will have three men back of a five-point block and is favored to break his board before he can extricate all of them. Like so many other tricky positions, this play involves risks, of course. My visceral aversion to the one point may be affecting my play here, but in spite of the danger White should welcome delay in the hope that he can hold his block while Red destroys his board. If the blots on W1 and W2 are hit, they will both be back in play and become useful later on. By far the best one for White would be to go from W8 to W7. He is after W4, not W1, and by being hit he actually increases his chances of making W4 later on, or perhaps W10.

Another purpose of this problem is to emphasize the importance of not playing impulsively. Too often beginners see a routine move, play it fast without thinking it through and wind up with an inferior choice. Whether or not you agree that it is correct to leave those two blots on W1 and W2, doing so should at least be considered. Always try to be aware of all your options; you don't have to play every move in a rush.

I would make this play under any conditions, tournament or money, regardless of the pressure involved.

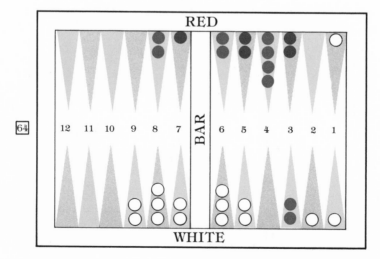

White to play 6–1.

71

Red is poised to make R4, or surely R2 if he fails on R4. There is great danger in coming up to R4 with the three, but if White takes a moment to think, he will realize that he doesn't even have a problem!

Why include this position, then? Because it is a fine example of tactics, the ability to anticipate and realize what will probably happen if White plays the three to R4. First of all, assume that Red rolls a superb shot — 3 – 2, for example. He points on White on R4 (which, of course, is vastly superior to hitting and covering R2). But even if White *knew* that Red was going to roll that 3 – 2, he should still play the same three! (The two can be played from W8 to W6.) If he had remained on R1 he would have had to advance his front men next time unless he was lucky enough to get a 6 – 1. But by letting himself be pointed on, he may stay on the bar and not disturb his board. It will now be up to Red to get those two back men out before breaking his board, and the odds are much against his doing so.

Try to evaluate these positions so that when a welcome number is rolled, you don't have to ponder over it and can play it as fast as you would remove four men if you rolled 6 – 6 while bearing off.

The temptation to play the three from W8 to W5, creating another bidder for W3, must be overcome. White may not have another chance to activate his back men, and big numbers will advance his board too fast. It is true that Red may produce a pair of 6 – 2's back to back, but if this happens you'll just have to pay off with — or without — a smile.

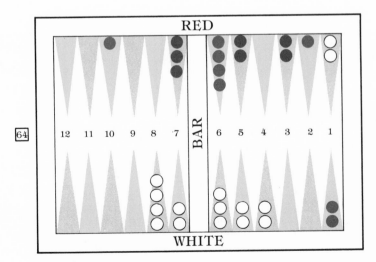

White to
play 3 – 2.

72

White has doubled and has a good chance for a gammon, but what a crime he would be committing if he used this 6 – 3 to point on W2. If left alone, Red may secure either W2 or W3, but how can he play a back game from there with his home board so far advanced? White should move his man on W12 all the way to W3, leaving a blot on that point. How can he take such a risk against Red's strong board? Because Red's board is about to collapse unless he rolls a 6 – 2 or 6 – 1 and escapes. Once Red's board is gone, White can start assaulting him in his own home board, but not until this happens.

If you have thought this problem through, imagine for a moment that you are Red. Wouldn't you like to have White point on you on W2? You would be on the bar, and if you didn't roll a three or one, you could hold your front block. White might get high numbers and have to break W7 before he released his back man. Red's strength is largely a mirage *provided* that he is allowed to play, so the unforgivable sin here would be to help him by hitting and enabling him to keep his position.

Finally, White's gammon chances are actually increased by letting Red play; he may hit another man if Red has to break his board.

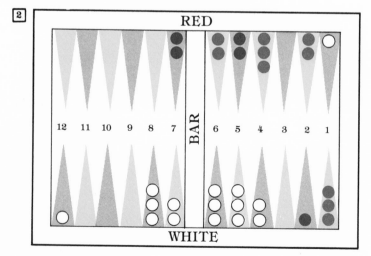

White to play 6 – 3.

73   This position shows the importance of timing. White has been doubled and has very little going for him. Red has both five points and much better timing. If you were White would you consider this 5 – 1 a good shot? Don't reply that you would have preferred double 5's; life is rarely that easy. Your answer should be that it is a good shot. What White needed to survive was a five so that he could release one of his men on R2 and keep his partially effective front block. Notice that nothing is duplicated; Red needs ones, twos and fives to hit and fours and sixes to escape from W5. Never mind; this is a moment when you don't worry about duplication. Come out with that five, and for want of anything else bravely start W9 with the one.

The main purpose of this problem is to show how wrong it would be to play safe from W10 to W4. There would go your last spare man, and if you didn't roll a five next time your outside block would begin to disintegrate. Also, Red might roll 5 – 2 or 2 – 2 to make R7, and then only a 6 – 1 would help you.

This is a study in tactics. If you thought seriously about coming out but rejected it because of the awkward one (it's too rash to split to R3), you are on your way, but if you never even considered coming out, you must pause and try to reevaluate such positions. If you study the whole situation, you will realize what a godsend that five is. You really have no problem here. Your position is bad, to be sure, but you are still breathing after this roll.

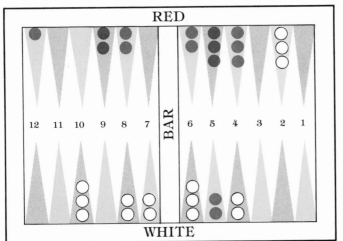

White to play 5 – 1.

74

If White hadn't come in, he surely would have been doubled. With no anchor, a man on the bar and three other blots around the board, he would have been forced to drop. But he enters with the three, and now must decide which of three R blots to hit with the five. He could hit inside on W4, but should reject doing so; if Red gets a four, he will almost certainly hit twice if he can, and with two men up, his board is formidable. Therefore White should choose between hitting on R8 or W8. Which is correct?

First of all, if you are White what is your primary objective here? You have in fact two objectives: you want to establish a defense in Red's strong board, and you wish to improve your own by making W4. With this in mind, you can see that hitting on W8 is vastly superior to R8. One reason is that by so doing White will have men on R3, R2 and R1, which gives him far more chances to establish one of these than if he had left R3 for R8. Another is that by hitting on W8, he creates another builder to work on W4 if Red should fail to secure it.

To be sure, by playing as suggested White leaves a fifth blot, whereas only four would be vulnerable if he hit on R8, but in the circumstances this is irrelevant. Sometimes leaving even one blot is not recommended, yet here it is suggested to the reader that he open a fifth one in a very dangerous position. Which only proves how difficult backgammon can be. It is all but impossible to generalize about it; each position must be analyzed afresh because, though many look alike, they may demand entirely different handling.

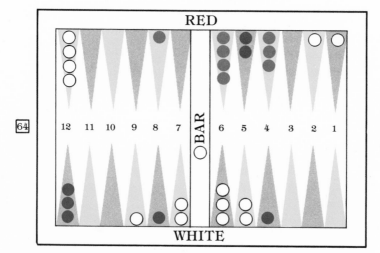

White to play 5 – 3. He is on the bar.

75

White has no good 4 – 1. He could play safe from his bar, but such cowardice would probably be punished later on, for he is completely stripped in his outer board. Most players, realizing this, would decide that there was nothing better than to hit on W1; after all, they have to leave a shot somewhere, and ones would be duplicated, Red needing that number to hit back or to make R3. Often this concept is correct; time and again positions will arise where the best tactics are to hit somewhere to create a diversion and keep your opponent busy for your own protection.

That's why this position is so interesting; it requires completely different tactics. What if Red is hit and doesn't come in? Is White any better off? Hardly. Further, if Red enters on a high point he can play that same man and keep W5. What White should be aware of – always be alert to your opponent's problems – is that Red is fast becoming stripped too. Therefore it should be White's objective to force Red to break either W5 or W12. How can he do this? Nothing is sure, but by far his best chance is to play two men from W8, adding to W7 and starting W4. Red would need a three to hit, or a four to come up to W5. But – and here is the strength of White's move – notice Red's predicament if he rolls any number, particularly a large one, that doesn't include a three or a four. He will have to break either anchor or else weaken his board.

Another plus for White in making this play is that he now has an extra man to cover W4, and if he is not hit, this point is of course infinitely more valuable than W1.

The more you look at this position the more you can be sure that it is the right play. Try to have a purpose behind each move, especially the complicated ones. Don't simply make plays that are standard procedure in many situations but are irrelevant in the actual position at hand.

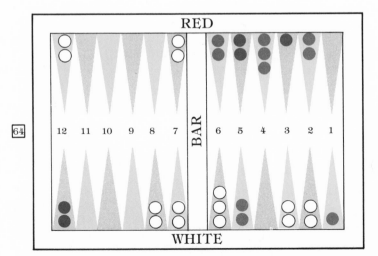

White to
play 4 – 1.

76

White is happy to have rolled a low number so that he can enter and secure some kind of defense. Since Red has a strong board, many players would enter on R1 and play the two from W6 to W4, thereby leaving only the man on R2 open. Alternatively, putting three men on R2 is safest, but White would now be dependent on rolling immediate fives, since he is stripped in his outer board. This is a fine example of tactics. White doesn't have to worry about his safety right now. He has R7, and with this 2 – 1 he can make R2, giving him fine balance. R2 is infinitely more valuable than R1, because it hampers the men on R8. If the passive play of entering on R1 and playing to W4 is selected, the blot on R2 can too easily be attacked. The one should be played from W6 to W5, leaving a blot.

Once again the natural aversion to leaving a voluntary double shot would deter a lot of players. But this fear must be overcome, because positions arise continually where such tactics are correct. White can use delay, which he will have if hit; if he is not, he has a chance to make W5 and form a strong board.

Set up this position and make the suggested play. Now, before Red rolls, look at the fluidity of White's game, and compare it with either of the other possible plays. To start W5 is not being particularly daring; it is merely playing the roll to the best possible advantage. Even though vulnerable on one point (W5), White's overall game is strong if the 2 – 1 is played the suggested way.

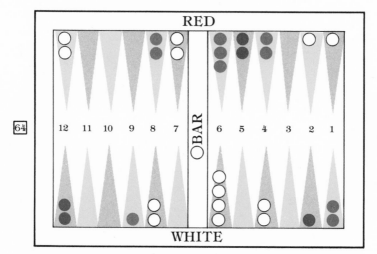

RED

64

12 11 10 9 8 7 BAR 6 5 4 3 2 1

WHITE

White to play 2 – 1. He is on the bar.

77

This problem is a lesson in priorities and logic. Of course 6 – 1 is a great shot for White. He could make his bar, forming a strong four-point block and threatening a prime, but then his blot on R4 would be extremely vulnerable. Note that any number by Red would hit conveniently except for sixes and ones, yet 6 – 1 specifically would hit on W8. Much as White would like to secure W7, it is hardly worth opening W8 and leaving his man on R4 defenseless. Therefore it must be correct to play the six out to R10 and leave W7 open. Freeing his back man is White's first priority.

Now White has to play a one, but he must think it through; it would be easy to become lax here and leap to the wrong conclusion. He has two choices; he can leave himself vulnerable to 6 – 6 or 6 – 5, but he can't protect against both. It is twice as likely that 6 – 5 will be rolled, so it would seem correct to leave a 6 – 6 shot. But here is where White must concentrate. If he leaves a 6 – 6 shot and is hit, Red has all but won the game. But if he leaves a 6 – 5 shot and is picked up, White has many return shots because Red will not yet have released his other back man. Finally, if White leaves a 6 – 5 shot and Red rolls 6 – 6, White remains in command because he would still be ahead in a race.

Thus, on balance, leaving a 6 – 5 is best. This way nothing beats you outright, whereas, though leaving a 6 – 6 is twice as safe, if you are hit, Red would almost surely win. A small but important difference, but it's a fine example of the disciplined thinking that is so vital in this game.

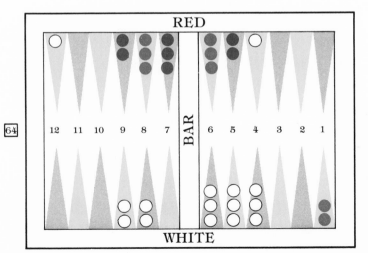

White to play 6 – 1.

78

Despite his overloaded five point, Red's timing is superior. White would like to contain those back men on W3 and could secure a four-point block by making W7. Many would choose this play, but to abandon the midpoint at this stage, thereby conceding the whole outfield, cannot be correct. White has a very good temporizing move here: he should come out to R8 with the six, and split to W5 with the one. The blot created on R8 is vulnerable to a five or a two and the one on W8 is duplicated by the five. Hence, unless Red rolls double 5's, he will not break his anchor and, instead, will hit the man on R8.

At this stage the game is very even, and White must keep his communication lines open between R4 and R12. To break the latter might be all right later on if a five-point block confronted Red's two men on W3, but not now.

This is another example of the correct tactic of leaving a voluntary double shot in the outer board. Too often such a play is rejected without its value being considered. Try to learn when these risks should be taken. There are far more opportunities for such moves than is realized, because players are naturally averse to leaving a single shot, and are actually horrified at leaving two.

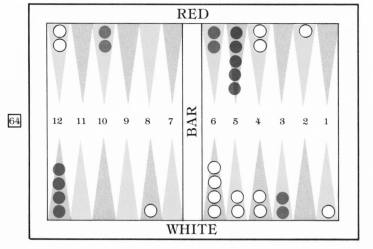

White to
play 6 – 1.

79

White has already doubled, and everything is going his way. He has the opposing five point, two of Red's men on the bar and a fine three-point board. This 4 – 3 is not difficult, but care must be taken not to squander it. Do not hit on R11 from R4! This looks obvious, but it would give Red a welcome respite. What he needs badly is any point as a defense in White's board. White should first bring a builder to W9, which bears on W3 in case Red should enter a man there. The three is optional; either start W10 or put a man on W5, creating another builder to hit on W1 if Red fails to secure that point. Under no circumstances make R4. You are all offense here, and don't need to be concerned with making points in your opponent's board.

It might reasonably be argued, "Why not hit on W1, since the objective is to blitz Red?" Because you are too short of builders; you are not ready for such tactics. If you had plenty of spare men in your outer board, perhaps you should do this, but not here. I believe the best play is to start the two outside points; though technically the man on W10 isn't a builder, it will be the next time, and it may be useful in making the bar if this point is needed (for example, if Red rolls a one). The object for White here is not to let Red get his bearings; he should mount an all-out attack to build up his board, and to hit on W1 if Red happens to stay out for a couple of rolls.

Try to familiarize yourself with these positions, which occur frequently. It would be criminal to hit on R11 or to make R4. I don't know which is worse; solve the question by doing neither.

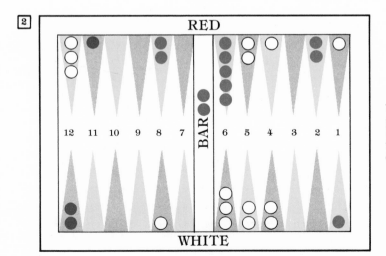

| 12 | 11 | 10 | 9 | 8 | 7 | BAR | 6 | 5 | 4 | 3 | 2 | 1 |

White to play 4 – 3. Red has two men on the bar.

80

The one is forced; White must enter on R1 and then play a six. His position is desperate, but he should keep his wits about him and be aware of one vital fact. Due to the score, if he fails to win this game he will be hardly worse off being gammoned than losing one point. In the latter case it will be 14 – 13 in his favor but his opponent will double immediately, so that the next game will be for the match. If he loses a gammon now, the score will be 14 – 14 and one more game will still decide. Realizing this, White should bravely hit Red on W5 with the six instead of playing to W1 in a frantic effort to save a gammon. He is in grave trouble, but need not give up. If Red rolls 2 – 2, 6 – 6 or 6 – 2, an 8 – 1 chance, he will not be able to enter and White will at least have an opportunity to turn the tables and win. The point here is to be aware of the possibilities available. It takes very little courage to make a daring play which costs nothing should it go wrong, but it is vital to be familiar with every factor so that you have the know-how to make such plays in the right situation.

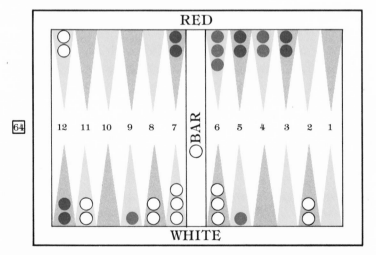

RED

| 12 | 11 | 10 | 9 | 8 | 7 | BAR | 6 | 5 | 4 | 3 | 2 | 1 |

WHITE

64

White to play
6 – 1 from the bar.
He is ahead 14 – 12
in a 15-point match,
Crawford Rule* apply

*The Crawford Rule, which is often used in tournament or match play, states that when either opponent gets to within one point of victory, the doubler may not be used in the next game *only*.

81

There are plenty of other numbers that White would prefer, but he has two reasonable plays: (A) make W3, hitting Red; (B) make R7 as a defensive measure. If he chooses (B) he will have to leave W9 and W5 open. Any even number will hit, plus 5 – 3, 5 – 1, 3 – 1 and 1 – 1. Thus, the only two that miss are 5 – 5 and 3 – 3, a 17 – 1 shot. These apparently suicidal odds would impel many players to choose (A) as the only sensible move.

But in spite of the overwhelming probability of being hit, I would select (B). Red has his valuable five point, and White must erect some defense to offset this edge. To make your opponent's bar point early is much stronger than is generally believed — especially when you have little else on either side of the board. To make W3 here still leaves three men open, though admittedly not as vulnerable. What is more important, however, is that (A) doesn't strengthen White's overall position enough. If R7 is made White has established a lifeline between his back men and the rest of his forces. Though he fully expects to be hit, no shot (except perhaps double 4's) is a disaster.

This problem also demonstrates the sound tactic of setting up some kind of a defense early in the game. The importance of this cannot be overemphasized, especially if you are less experienced or proficient in technique than your opponent.

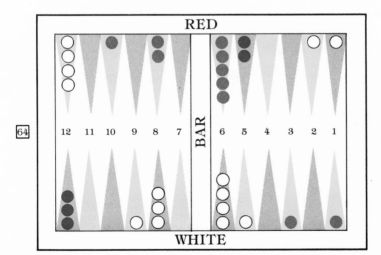

White to
play 6 – 5.

82

The game has reached a critical stage. White wanted a six in order to make W7, but this 5 – 2 is not a disaster. He has several choices, the best of which is to make R3 and start W3. This has two purposes; if Red can release his man on W1, White wants to be hit because he will then be committed to a back game and can use all the delay possible. Handling the 5 – 2 this way also assures White that Red must play, and if he should roll 3 – 3, 4 – 4, 5 – 5 or 6 – 6 he must seriously weaken his near prime. To hit on W1 would be a mistake because Red might not reenter, and to save the blots on W12 or W7 would be pointless.

The back-game concept is graphically demonstrated here. White leaves blots on W3, 7, 8 and 12 plus his lone man on R1 (which point he hopes to establish should one or more of the other blots be hit). Most players would make R3 but wouldn't consider starting W3. However, this part of the move is vital, for if it is not done, Red might escape with his back man without hitting. If this happened, White's timing would be in jeopardy and 5 – 5 or 4 – 4, for instance, plus most other high numbers would destroy him. Remember that if you have two solid points in your opponent's board in a back game, plus a potential third, your priority is to keep your men in play at all costs. No matter how many are hit and sent back they all remain in play.

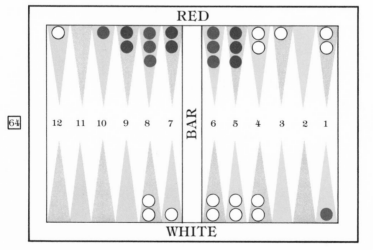

RED

64

12 11 10 9 8 7 BAR 6 5 4 3 2 1

WHITE

White to play 5 – 2.

83

As is so often the case, White here has an aesthetic play: cover W9, forming an important block, and save the blot on R12. This is neat and orderly, but it brands the perpetrator of such a move as an intermediate or beginner by showing a serious lack of understanding in passing up a precious opportunity. White should hit twice in his board, sending both of Red's men to the bar and leaving a blot on his two point.

There are many reasons to be aggressive here. White has his valuable five point, which may impede Red's reentry. Also this play protects White's blots on R4 and R2 from attack because Red will have to reenter before developing his inner board. Moreover, if he gets a two and sends White to the bar, White will have an excellent chance to secure R5 and thus hold both five points.

To make the recommended play White must break W8 leaving a total of seven blots around the board! This fact would deter many people, but if you consider the position, these blots are hardly a liability. All are "working" except perhaps the man on W2, and if Red rolls even a single five or a six and not a two on the next roll, he will be hard pressed to accept a double.

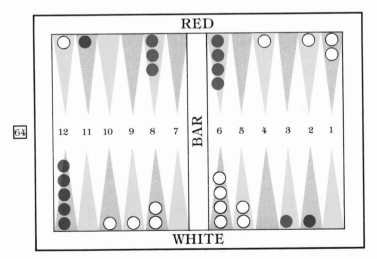

White to
play 5 – 1.

84

This is a comparatively simple problem, and yet many different solutions would be offered if it were put to a panel. Red has a man up and owns the cube. White has a 5 – 3 to play.

To save the blot on R4, leaving Red with only a 6 – 3 to hit, is tempting and in certain situations is probably correct. For example, if you are at 14 – 14 in a fifteen-point tournament match it would be reasonable. But in a money game White should be more aggressive because of the gammon possibility. Either make W3, leaving Red some combination shots or go all out and hit Red on W1 from W6 and play the three in from W8 to W5, leaving a maximum number of builders. Which of these latter plays is correct? No one can be sure; no group of experts would agree 100 percent either way. But such situations—and they are not really complicated—are what makes this game so inscrutable. Hunches are all right to follow as long as you don't defy percentages to play them; here is a position where you should follow that hunch.

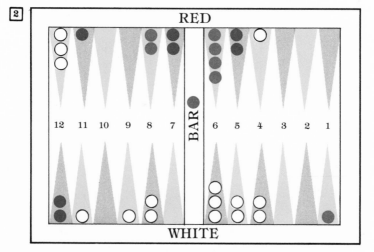

White to play 5 – 3.

85

White must come in on R5 and has three choices for the one. He can move his blot on R10 to R11, start W7 or start W4. Red is ahead of himself but has a four-point board and is threatening to blitz White. White has two men exposed already and doesn't relish exposing a third, but in this position he should do so. The correct play is to start W4, duplicating threes, the same number White is vulnerable to on R10 and R5. Red will do all in his power to hit White on his next turn and if White should move to R11 — as many would, so as not to leave yet another blot — all he would be doing would be to leave himself vulnerable to a two, in addition to the three and the one already menacing him on R5. White's priority at this moment is to leave the least number of shots, and starting W4 accomplishes this. The position gives Red a total of twenty-four shots, but if White had moved to R11 he would have left twenty-eight shots and starting W7 would leave thirty-one. White has already been doubled and his object here is to survive; starting W4 is not brave, but is simply common sense. The extra man exposed by this play is a mirage, because if White fails to establish a point somewhere and is blitzed, the two men sent to the bar will cost him a gammon in any case. In other words, Red doesn't need the third man.

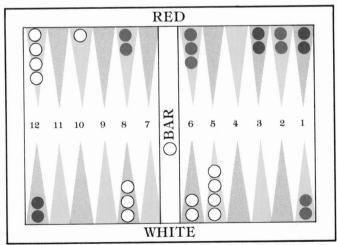

RED

WHITE

12 11 10 9 8 7 BAR 6 5 4 3 2 1

White to play 5 – 1. He is on the bar.

2

86

Red has had the best of the early going, and is poised to make either R8 or R4 which will seriously hinder White's back men in their attempt to escape. White must mount some kind of defense or counterattack. He has no better four than covering W9 and now has to select a one. He could split to R2, which many would do and is not unreasonable, but it is risky with all those builders trained on him; if pointed on or hit twice he runs the danger of being blitzed. He should therefore start W7. If Red hits with a six, he cannot also lock White in further by improving his board. This principle is constantly occurring in the middle game and should be understood fully. It is true that starting W7 allows Red complete freedom to make R4 or R8, but if either of these happens, White will not have been disturbed on W7 and is a prohibitive favorite to make his bar and form a strong counterblock.

To sum up: White must take positive action. It is much the best to start W7. Splitting to R2 is extremely risky, but I would not argue strongly against it. The unpardonable play would be to move from W6 to W5, which is safe and risks nothing but deserves to—and probably would—lose by default.

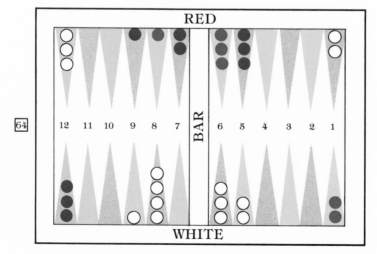

White to
play 4–1.

87

Red has a reasonable back game but is too far advanced. This 5 – 1 is a good shot for White, putting a builder on W7 and giving him excellent balance. The question is, Should White hit en passant on W12? It is a safe move, but it allows Red valuable delay. If White does not hit, Red conceivably could cause trouble by rolling 1 – 1 or 3 – 1, thereby hitting and making a four-point board. Of course White would welcome being hit with 5 – 4 or 6 – 3, for Red would be asking to lose a gammon if he ventured such a play. However, even if Red rolls a 1 – 1 or 3 – 1, Red would still face a mammoth task in containing the blot he has just hit while extricating those four men from White's board. It could happen—almost anything can in backgammon—but the odds are very much against it. By far the stronger play for White is to ignore Red's blot and move to W7 without hitting.

Often in a position like this the player foresees possible disaster if he doesn't hit, but fails to analyze the whole picture. Remember that in essence the game is a series of calculated risks; here is an excellent example of when to take one.

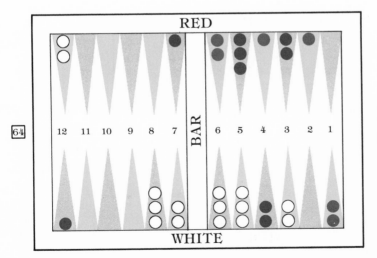

White to
play 5 – 1.

88

White must enter on R4 and then consider his other three fours. The crux of this position is centered on R4, the vital point that both sides want to capture. How best to secure it? White would like to do something constructive with this throw, but by doing so he would leave his blot on R4 too vulnerable. His best play is to hit twice from R12 to W1, leaving a blot there. Red will have to ignore R4 at least for this roll (unless he rolls a double), and even if he hits White on W1 and enters both men, White will have an excellent opportunity to secure R4. Without this point White can hardly survive, so he must direct all his attention to it.

This move surely has no aesthetic value and it seems as if White is squandering a powerful roll, but he has no time to do anything else. It is a matter of priorities, and for the moment all other plays are less important than securing an anchor on R4.

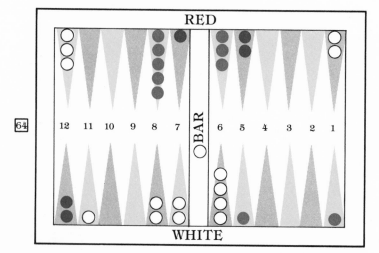

RED

64

12 11 10 9 8 7 BAR 6 5 4 3 2 1

WHITE

White to play 4–4. He is on the bar.

89

This 6–6 is a perfect shot for White. He covers W2 from R5 with three of his sixes, making a prime, and now has to decide what to do with the fourth. He can establish R7, retaining his prime, or he can hit on W1, putting another of Red's men on the bar. Most people would resolve this decision by making R7, unless a gammon was vital. It looks reasonable to do this, but here is a position where White's offense is so strong that he should abandon his defense for an all-out attack, using the fourth six to hit on W1. Not only is it the right play for a gammon, but it is the right play under all circumstances. If Red is allowed to establish on W1, he will have a strong game and can be a threat until the end. Double ones by Red might be a disaster for White, but it is well worth the risk.

In most games a critical position arises somewhere along the line when it is vital to take advantage of an opportunity. Here is such a position. If to hit seems too rash here, put yourself in Red's shoes. Under *any* circumstances—tournament, chouette or head-to-head—wouldn't you sigh with relief if White made R7 and allowed you a chance to establish R1? This kind of reasoning can often aid you in making the correct play.

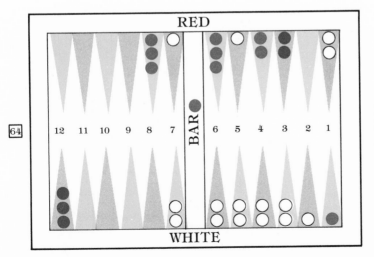

White to play 6–6. Red is on the bar.

90

Here is a position that can be argued at length. There are two alternatives: either hit on R7 or make W4. Both plays have merit, and each could be right or wrong depending on Red's next roll. There is no way either can be judged clearly superior. However, I have a strong preference for making W4. R7 is not as important because R5 is open, and since White's timing is so good, he can afford to make the play that may destroy Red's timing. A 5–5 or 6–6 roll by Red would be a disaster, and any high number would be unwelcome. If Red was certain to make R5, White should hit, but White's strong four-point block, with five men ready on R12 to add to it, is convincing evidence that the non-hitting play is best. A problem like this enhances the mystery of the game, because no doubt many will be adamant in favor of hitting.

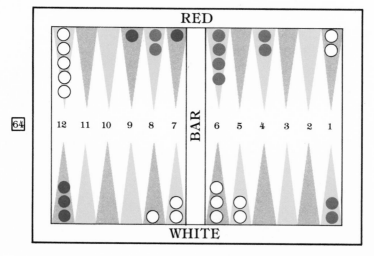

White to play 4–2.

91

Red's timing is excellent and it is going to be difficult for White to play a blocking game, so his best chance is an all-out back game. The double 1's give him great flexibility. He should make R2 with two of his ones, and then hit twice on W7 and W4, splitting off W8 and W5 to do so. White wants to force his opponent to hit him, and Red must do so if he rolls a five or four. Most players would enter on R2 and hit with the builder on R6, keeping a semblance of a block. Such tactics are incorrect. White's sole concern is delay; he must slow down, and hitting once off the six point is not likely to force Red to hit him.

The best points to hold in a back game are the two and three. (Here White holds one, two and three.) For the moment this is fine, but when Red gets all his men around and is ready to bring them in, White should break R1 with a one or two. This seemingly foolish move forces Red to play fives and sixes, which could be awkward; these would be unplayable if R1 wasn't broken.

The suggested play may seem unnatural, but once again common sense dictates it. Red has a lot of time to get around, and White must do all he can to keep his men in play.

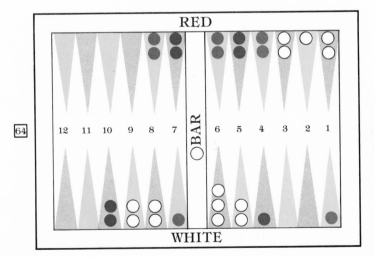

White to play 1 – 1 from the bar.

92   The game is in its early stages, but already White's timing is bad for a back game and he must resist the urge to hold both R1 and R2. Instead, he should attack by starting R7 with the six. The best play for the one is to make R2 instead of starting R3, as many would do. The latter play invites being hit twice and gives Red a possible tempo if White rolls a six next time with two men on the bar. Red will probably hit White on R7, but he may not be able to secure the point. White then will have an excellent opportunity to make a forward point in Red's board or to hit back. On the other hand, if Red fails to hit, White will be a big favorite to make R7. Even though a substantial risk is involved, not to attack the rival bar point in positions like this shows a lack of good tactics. Many people would play the six from R12 to W7, and then look around for a one. Such a play is being too kind to your opponent. Remember that White has W5, which Red must respect, and he must create a diversion to deter Red from strengthening his advantage.

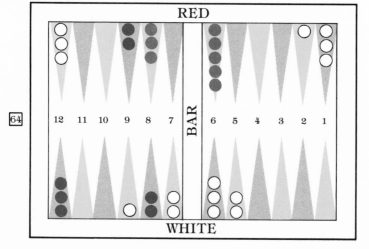

White to
play 6–1.

93

Red has just failed to enter, and White, seeing a chance for a blitz, doubles. Red accepts and White rolls 3–2. Two natural plays, which the majority would prefer, are to make W7, or both W10 and W9. In the first case a good point is made, and in the latter two points, and at the same time some of the six blots that White has strewn all over the landscape are made safe. But both of these plays show a weakness in strategy. Red is on the bar, and making either of the above plays in no way hinders him from entering. There are many numbers he can roll where he can enter and hit one of White's blots. If this happens, both sides are in a slugfest, with the game up for grabs. However, if White analyzes his position in depth, he will appreciate the necessity of hitting on W1 with his 3–2, putting a second man of Red's on the bar. Paradoxically, by exposing yet another man, White tends to protect all his blots with this play, because, with two men up, Red can do nothing to make points (unless he gets a double), and if he fails to roll a one or a double he will be in jeopardy of losing a gammon. If White could have made W5 or W4, there would be much to recommend doing so, but at this juncture W7 is a mirage, and worth practically nothing.

This position demonstrates basic strategy: the ability to size up what your real purpose is. In addition, it is a concrete example of how overrated your own bar point can be, especially early in the game.

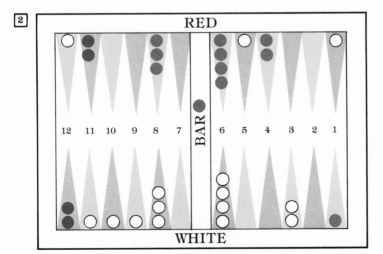

White to play 3–2. Red is on the bar.

94 This is not an easy decision. The choice is either to cover W3 from W8 and hit on W2 with the four, or to go out all the way with one man from R5 to W11. There is a good case for both plays. Most people would prefer (A), on the theory that since a shot must be left in any case, why not hit? But if Red does get a two, White is in danger of losing a gammon because W8 is now vulnerable. If (B) is selected and Red gets a one, hitting the man on W3, he may later be able to pick up the blot left on W11 and win a gammon here too. The subtle advantage in (B), however, is that if Red does hit on W3, he has not necessarily escaped from White's grasp, because he needs either a four or a six with the one to accomplish this. Moreover, he will have to play any other number than a four or six to his disadvantage on his side of the board because he is stripped there. Further, if (B) is chosen and Red fails to roll a one or a five, he must weaken his front position. To run from R5 to W11 may not seem aggressive enough, but always remember that in backgammon there are countless positions with a built-in potential for self-destruction if left alone. Passive, not active, treatment is required, and on balance (B) is better for just this reason. There is a satisfaction in watching your opponent commit suicide, and here is a good chance to let him do so.

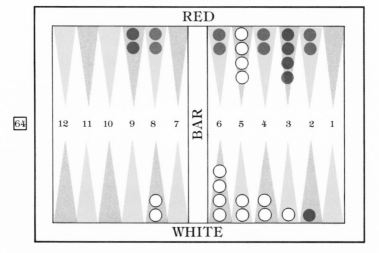

RED

64 | 12 11 10 9 8 7 BAR 6 5 4 3 2 1

White to play 5 – 4.

WHITE

95

White must enter on R3 and then choose between two fives. R4 is a valuable point for White to have, but this game is unusual because Red is threatening to take command of the whole outfield. White's men are badly placed, and soon sixes may be embarrassing for him. To move the five from W6 to W1 is tempting, and many would do so in order to hold R4. But such a play must be rejected; not only is the builder vital but to go to W1 would only be marking time and making matters worse. White should reluctantly abandon R4 and come out to R9, thereby bidding to secure an outfield point. Leaving three blots on Red's potentially strong home board is not as hazardous as it appears. That Red may roll a small double is a risk White must take, and if Red rolls any six, five or one he can't wound White mortally. Moreover, the very fact that there are three blots gives White a better chance of covering at least one of them if he is hit.

No one advocates defensive concepts more than this writer, but when a position like this arises, White must challenge and move forward. To re-trench here would give Red too much momentum, from which White might never recover.

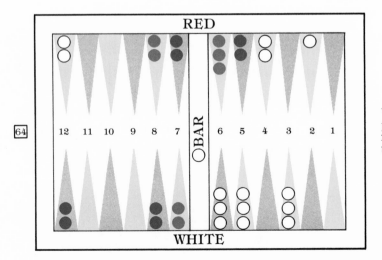

White to play 5–3 from the bar.

96

This is one of the easiest problems in the book, but it is interesting because of the type of player who would choose either of the two possibilities. White must enter both men on R1, and now has to decide: (A) whether to make W5, hitting; or (B) to establish R2. The correct move under all conditions is (A). No expert would pause for a moment, and, surprisingly, neither would a beginner. The intermediate player, however, who is at the stage where a "little learning is a dangerous thing," might be tempted by (B). Overall, White has bad timing for a back game. Secondly, when and if you do opt for a back game, try not to play from the one and two points. Your men look strong and solid back there, but unless the whole operation is timed perfectly—which is most difficult—they usually end up in disaster. Thirdly and most important, always seek to avoid back games if there is an option. Don't jump into one voluntarily.

Here White's five point is welcome, forming a four-point block and sending a man to the bar. It is true that White needs to diversify those four men on R1, but he will have a chance to do so on his next roll because Red is on the bar and cannot improve his board except with double 2's or double 4's. White should opt for a forward blocking game and his next immediate objective is to make R4. If his next roll is 3 – 1, he should start both R4 and R2. Red has no builders in his outer board and will have trouble thwarting White in his attempt to make a forward anchor.

The lessons of this problem are not to try to be fancy unless you are sure of what you are doing, and to keep away from back games in general, and the one- and two-point variety in particular.

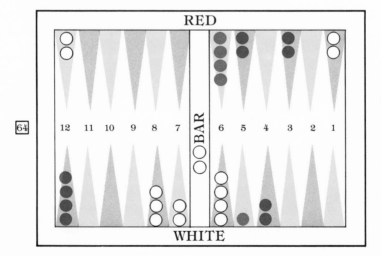

64

White to play 1 – 1. He has two men on the bar.

97

White has a reasonably well-timed back game. He is a bit far advanced, but he holds the best two possible points in his opponent's board. It is tempting to try to hold Red behind a five-point block by pointing on him on W4, and many would do so because it looks correct. But what if Red stays out? White will be compelled to rush his troops too far forward without being able to release his back men. Further, even if Red does enter on a low point, he has those men on R11 and R12 as reserves if he can't get out of White's board immediately.

White is not ready to play a blocking game; he must opt for an all-out back game. Thus, his best play is to move two men off W7, hitting on W4 and starting W3. This strategy is White's best because, in order to release his back man, Red must hit White somewhere. There is no number on the dice that allows Red to escape without hitting, and of course White welcomes being hit. He needs delay and, in fact, would like to stay on the bar for several rolls. At this juncture his paramount objective is to ensure that his forces are not removed from play — that is, far down on his board. If he is hit on W3, W4 or W7, it will help him to hold his position.

When playing a back game, always be on the alert for that moment when you can suddenly change to a blocking or holding game, but be sure of your ground. If you tried to do so here by making W4 with the 4 – 3 roll, you would be striking too soon and considerably lessening your opponent's problems.

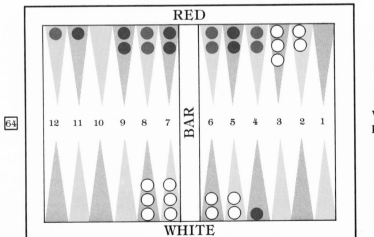

RED

64 12 11 10 9 8 7 BAR 6 5 4 3 2 1

WHITE

White to
play 4 – 3.

98

It would be interesting to know the percentage of backgammon players who would make W9 with this 5–4. Probably a majority of them. It is a bad roll; there is no way to save the blot on R11 without exposing another one on R12, and to come all the way out from R1 leaves too many men open. Therefore many would be resigned to making W9, creating a four-point block with the idea that there is nothing better to do. Certainly, those four points in a row do look nice structurally. (It is unfair and probably not true, but I would guess that as a group architects make bad backgammon players.)

The truth is that almost any other choice is superior to breaking R12. White could hit on W2 and move from R11 to W9, or he could point on W2. Even coming out to R10 from R1, though not recommended, is better than making W9 at the expense of giving up White's outfield. I have a slight preference for making W2. If Red stays on the bar, White has an excellent chance (it's only 5–4 against his doing so) of picking up Red's blot on R7, and he may then be able to improve his board, except for the bastion Red holds on W5, before his opponent can develop any offensive position. I don't fault hitting on W2 and starting W9, but categorically oppose breaking R12.

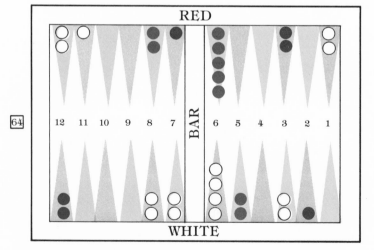

RED

64 | 12 11 10 9 8 7 | BAR | 6 5 4 3 2 1

WHITE

White to play 5–4.

99

Here is another doubling situation. In all money games, and if the players are of more or less even skills, White should double. Also in all chouettes, whether in the box or against it. The reason is that White has a great chance for a gammon. Red has four blots around the board as opposed to White's two, and White has four points covered in his board to three for his opponent. Still, if White fails to enter, he will probably be redoubled, and if so, he should drop. Thus, by doubling here, he risks two points for a possible four—obviously sound tactics,

On the other hand, if this identical position came up early in a tournament match between an expert and a comparative beginner, the expert should not double, unless he has read his opponent so well that he is sure the latter will drop. This is the kind of position in which the weaker player should *want* to be doubled, for it gives him leverage and leaves it up to the dice. Conversely, if the beginner is White against an expert Red, White should double like a shot and pray that Red takes it. The opportunity to win four points in a single game is a lure worth taking great risks for.

Once again, this position shows how subtle the use of the cube can be. Always try to be alert for gammon chances, especially against a better player. When such positions arise, exploit them by doubling boldly. You not only put respect into your opponent, but actually give yourself your best chance to beat him.

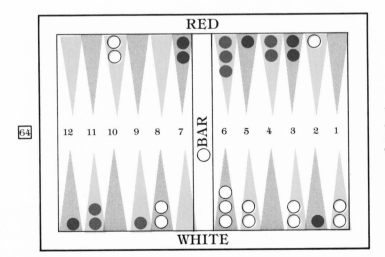

White is on the bar. Should he double?

100

This problem is not difficult if analyzed; it is simply a basic example of why a player must think before he moves. Watch out for succumbing to reflex actions without projecting ahead. Here White, if he is merely banging his men around, might easily fall into a trap. One of the first lessons is to make points whenever possible, and here two builders are perfectly placed to allow White not only to hit, but also to secure a five-point board. He reasons that Red may spend a long time on the bar, and that a gammon is not out of the question. This is a good time to reiterate the fact that when you are on the bar attempting to enter your opponent's five-point board, the odds are 25 – 11 against you, but that on two rolls you become a slight favorite to do so. Since Red is going to have many more than two rolls to get a five, he is a favorite to come in long before White can get all his men around.

What White should realize here is that if he ignores Red on W1 and comes out to R7 instead, Red will be forced to break W5 or W12, or else ruin his already flimsy board – unless, of course, he rolls a four, and the odds are 25 – 11 against this. If White makes W1 and Red stays on the bar, he holds his position and remains a threat. Further, if Red reenters immediately on W5, he can play this same man from that point and keep the rest of his forces intact.

What it comes down to is that White must give Red every chance to destroy his position, not preserve it. By pointing on W1, he is helping his opponent.

On the other hand, the final irony of this position, and what makes this such an infuriating game, is that every once in a while White will unthinkingly make W1 and send Red to the bar, where he will remain for roll after

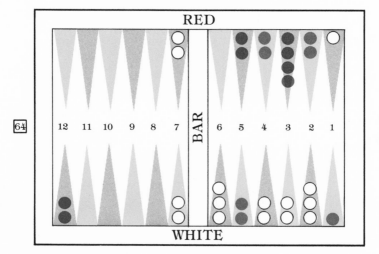

64

White to
play 5 – 1.

roll as White roars around into his board and bears all his men off, winning a gammon with ease. And if it happens to be an important game which wins a tournament match, some spectators will congratulate White on how well he has played, and White will modestly agree!

101

White should be aware of Red's bad timing. Red is too advanced to play a back game, yet is hopelessly trapped in one. White must not help him by being bold here and hitting both on R7 and W3; rather, it should be his objective to let Red destroy himself by ruining his board. It may seem that W3 is important, but let Red make it; he can't hold it for long. The correct play is R1 to R7, hitting, and R1 to R2 for a defensive anchor. Hitting seems to contradict the strategy of letting Red play, and so it does in a way. But it is necessary for the moment in order to protect White's blot on W7, which he is a favorite to cover next time. He would then have a four-point block and builders coming around to add to it. Unless Red can release at least one man, his board will collapse, and in any case he can't hold his position for long.

This strategy by White is vastly superior to going for a blitz by hitting twice. Not only would that be dangerous — Red might roll a three and White could stay out a few rolls — but even if it succeeded and White closed his board except for W1, Red would maintain his strong board and be a threat to the very end. He would be playing an ace-point game, making him a big favorite to get a shot, and since his board would be intact, he could easily win if he hit.

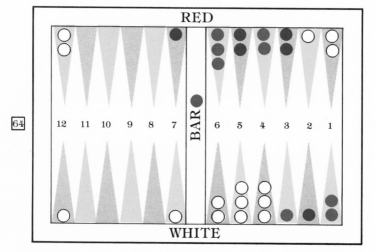

White to
play 6 – 1.
Red is
on the bar.

102

Red has next to nothing, and White has rolled a great shot but must be careful to get the most out of it. Red hasn't the shadow of a defense, so White's tactics should be all-out offense. When a fighter has his opponent reeling on the ropes, he doesn't think of covering up, but just throws punches.

The danger here is that White will overlook what his priorities are. What Red needs to survive is a point—any point—in White's board, so White should try to thwart him. Therefore the correct play is to enter on R3, bring a builder to W10, and transfer W5 to W2, hitting. This play may cause raised eyebrows, for the two point is hardly as valuable as the five point. But when you can put a second man on the bar and prevent a point being made, it is well worth it.

To play to W10 instead of hitting on R7 is basic. What is needed is another builder for W5; Red already has two men up and after filling his board, White can pick off the man on R7 at leisure. But not now! The builder is too valuable.

As is always the case in this volatile game, if Red replies with double 5's, White has lost his whole advantage. Double 3's and double 1's are also devastating, but when only three shots out of thirty-six hurt you—an 11–1 chance—you should take the risk. Watch for these situations; they crop up often. In a game like this, the *quantity*, not the *quality*, of points made is important. Make them in any order, but at all costs keep your opponent from establishing an anchor in your board. A blitz is your objective.

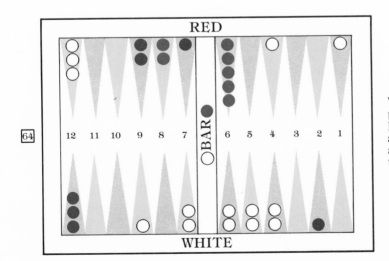

RED

64

12 11 10 9 8 7 BAR 6 5 4 3 2 1

WHITE

White to play 3–3. Both White and Red are on the bar.

103

White must enter on R1, hitting, and then has two reasonable fours: (A) start W9; (B) hit again on W4, leaving two blots in the board but putting a second Red man on the bar. Surprisingly, the risk is exactly the same; in both instances Red would be a 7 – 5 favorite to hit somewhere. He is perhaps a bit more likely to hit two men if (B) is selected; nevertheless I would choose this play. All other things being about equal, aggressiveness is better. Also, the move is more constructive; starting W9 is too passive, and a man there is almost as vulnerable in any case. Though in a precarious position, White is still breathing. If Red fails to hit, White has gained a valuable tempo, and if White is hit, his chances of establishing a point in Red's board are good.

This problem is important because it shows that hitting twice and leaving two open men in one's own board does not necessarily mean suicide. Such plays should be made more often than they are. Also, this position illustrates the mirages of the game; if asked which play — (A) or (B) — is more dangerous, the vast majority of players would say scornfully, "Why, (B) of course! Anyone can see that!"

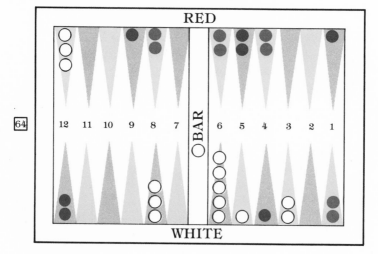

RED

64

12 11 10 9 8 7 BAR 6 5 4 3 2 1

WHITE

White to
play 4 – 1.
He is
on the bar.

104

This is not an easy decision. It is tempting to hit on W12 from R4. Red has no board, and this play not only releases a man but creates a builder for the bar or W10. But Red has a sound back game; the four and three points, though not as strong as the three and two, are formidable. Further, by hitting, White would be giving Red valuable delay. Indeed, Red wants another man back so that he can play from White's board without breaking either W3 or W4. White must do everything he can to speed up Red, not to stop him playing, so his best move here is to take both men down from R12 to W9 and W8. If Red then hits on W10, he will not only have lost his forward position in White's board, and be extremely vulnerable to his blot on W4 being pointed on, but also risks being picked up in his own board. Red needs a three or an eight to make R5, but White should take this risk.

Positions similar to this occur constantly in back games. The man defending against them—in this case White—must resist the temptation to make the easy move which for the moment leaves him in no peril. He should learn to look ahead and prepare now for future trouble. To hit here would show lack of strategy and foresight; it is not the correct tactic for the ultimate objective—winning the game. (I cannot resist adding here that if baseball's major-league managers played backgammon, all would go astray on a problem like this. To a man they consider only the immediate crisis, and never attempt to formulate overall strategy to win the game itself.)

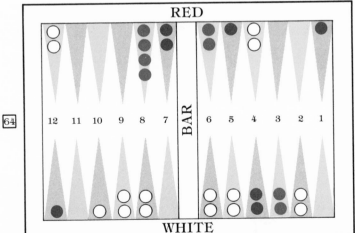

White to play 5 – 4.

105

There are two obvious choices — perhaps some would say only one: (A) make W10 with the blot on R11, and move the back man to R2; (B), the only other reasonable play, is to make W9, leaving a blot on R11. Which is better, and is it vital either way?

I have a strong preference for (B), but, quite honestly, I have no logical explanation. Call it instinct if you like, but I feel certain that (B) is correct. There is something awkward about W10, even though of course it is a worthwhile point, blocking sixes. White's position is besmirched by his having made his useless one point, and even though Red hasn't developed his board at all, White is going to have his hands full getting all his men safely home.

There is a world-renowned expert whom I like to needle by telling him that he makes more correct imaginative plays *without knowing why* than anyone else I know. He invariably replies, "I don't know whether I like the second half of that statement!" When I show him this position, I'd give odds that he will pick (B).

The consecutive points W9 and W8 seem superior to W10 and W8, but is this difference worth risking being hit on R11? Red has no board, to be sure, but White has only one more man to clear if he chooses (A). Yet I would select (B) under all conditions, and am not ashamed to confess that I don't know why!

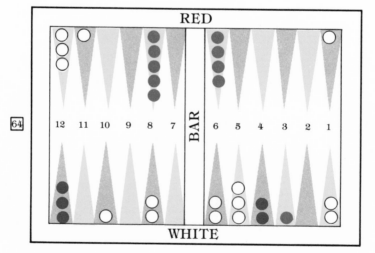

RED

64

12 11 10 9 8 7 BAR 6 5 4 3 2 1

WHITE

White to play 4 – 1.

106

White's timing is bad for a back game, and he hasn't yet established a second point in Red's board. In addition, he is behind a prime. But this 4 – 4 gives him a chance. To hit, cover W3, and make W4 might seem to be the obvious play, but what would it prove? White simply cannot waste time building his board now when he has four men captured. He must make every effort to establish R1 or R2 by forcing Red to hit. Therefore he should play R12 to W5, hitting, en route, W8 to W4, and W6 to W2. If nothing else, this is a colorful layout, with four blots in his board and one on his bar! Unless Red rolls a one or double 6's, he will be forced to hit, and he may have to hit twice in order to escape — just what White wants. If White can establish another back point in Red's board, he has a chance. (Of course Red is going for a gammon here, and White should drop if doubled; the gammon threat is simply too great.)

This play looks flamboyant, but it is far less daring than it seems. The danger lies in the fact that when hit, White may not reenter, and now Red will have a chance to point on the blots on R1 and R2, thereby thwarting any back game for White. But backgammon is a series of calculated risks, and this is a great opportunity for White to take a bold one in attempting to get back into the game.

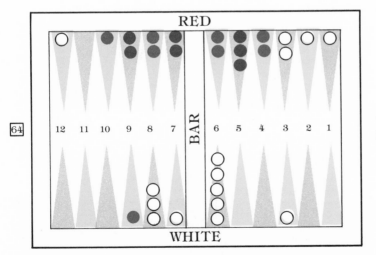

White to
play 4 – 4.

107

The five looks easy, but where's the six? Red's timing isn't perfect, but he has a reasonable back game. What White doesn't want is to hit any more of Red's men; still, if he covers W8, whatever six he plays will give Red a chance to hit and open more men, so that White may be forced to help his opponent's timing by hitting him again. Therefore White's best play is to move all the way from R1 to R12, leaving W8 open. Certainly, Red isn't ready to hit this blot with a five; he might do so with a six, but given his board this doesn't figure to help him much. And if Red fails to get a six, White may now make W8, containing him and perhaps forcing him to advance too fast and break his board.

This problem is an excellent example of the tactics in defending against a back game. It is usually easier to defend against than to play one, because timing is so vital for the offense. One large double at the wrong time can sabotage one's entire position. For example, suppose White eventually secures W8 after freeing his back man, and Red then rolls double 5's. He is all but destroyed, and will have to be very lucky to avoid a gammon.

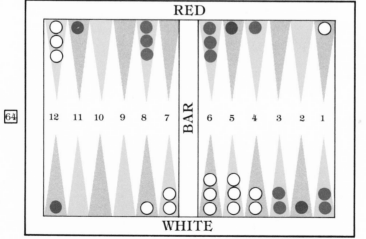

RED

64

12 11 10 9 8 7 BAR 6 5 4 3 2 1

WHITE

White to play 6–5.

108

It is very early, but Red already has a game far superior to White's. White must enter on R2 and has nothing better to do than to make a desperate move: starting R7. He isn't panicking; he is simply doing the best he can with what he has. Any other six would be craven and not help him at all. Starting R7 is very dangerous; he could be hit twice and possibly blitzed, but it is far and away his best play. If Red rolls a bad shot and doesn't hit, White has an excellent chance to cover, and if he secures R7, he has virtually equalized the game.

As a general principle it is wrong to break one's back men this early, especially when the player has no defense or no enemy men trapped; here both these conditions exist, yet, paradoxically, it is mandatory to break R1.

Incidentally, in many money games a daredevil Red might double after this play, seeing his opportunity for a blitz and possible gammon. Our advice would be to accept such a double; White stands an excellent chance of consolidating somewhere in Red's board, or perhaps on R7. Again the principle "When in doubt, take" should be followed. Surely there is a doubt here, and in the long run those who dropped would be losers.

In tournaments, however, the situation is different. If the score was 11 all in a fifteen-point match, it would be a superb double and White should drop, for he can't risk losing the match on this one game. This is another example of how doubling strategy differs markedly between tournament and money games.

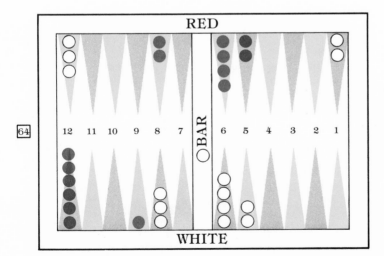

White to
play 6-2
from
the bar.

109

White has already doubled and has a chance for a gammon if he can pick up the blot on W11, because he already has one of Red's men on the bar. This is an easy problem, but there is something to be learned here; there are many such situations, and it is important to recognize them when they appear. With a four-point board White has Red on the bar; also, by playing the one to W9 he has two outside blocks. What better time to leave R5? That bastion has served its purpose well, but now is the time for White to try to get those two men home while his opponent's striking power is curtailed.

How many people would play the six to W4 for a builder? Probably quite a few; it's safe, and the builder is in play and valuable. Yet not to come out here, to sit back and pray for a nine or a big double, is simply not realistic. When an opportunity arises you must seize it; you may not get another. Most of the time your decision will be tougher than this one. Notice that Red needs threes and twos to enter, and also threes and twos to hit on R11; further, if Red rolls any six, five or four (or double 1's) he cannot touch you. So the odds are $3\frac{1}{2}-1$ that you won't be hit, and even if you are, there are return shots (barring a miracle roll like double 3's). Usually the odds won't be as much in your favor in such situations, so harden yourself to take these calculated risks.

This position actually occurred in a tournament in Nassau. White made the correct play, but Red came in with double 2's, White stayed out, and Red deliberately did not redouble, boldly going for the gammon and getting it. Those four points turned the match around both numerically and psychologically. Afterwards many players castigated White for his "bad" move. This will always happen, of course, but White knew better, even though it was small consolation for losing the match.

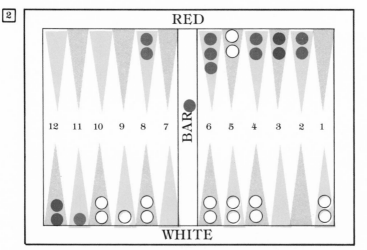

White to
play 6-1.
Red is
on the bar.

110

Considering the fact that White has been doubled, he is in pretty good shape, and this 6–4 gives him options. He can play safe by making W2, or by moving a man to W3 from R12. Red has a good board and White does not want to be hit, so one of these plays is tempting. He also can cover W4 and hit on W12 from R7. This is bold because it gives up his defense, even though only an indirect shot is left; Red first has to come in from the bar. If this play is chosen, White is giving Red sixteen return shots. A third choice would be to cover W4 and start W7, leaving a two shot.

White must realize that he has very good timing, much better than Red's, and therefore he should reject hitting. One reason is that even if he is not hit back on the next shot, he is still far from home. By refusing to hit, he is thus retaining his strong defense on R7, and since he has chosen to retain this strategic point, he can well afford to start W7, leaving a two shot, and to cover W4.

A problem like this is the essence of backgammon. It isn't really difficult; all it takes is a succession of logical steps. For example, slotting on W7 makes White vulnerable to only eleven shots, whereas if he hits on W12 he can be hit with sixteen. Further, even if he hits on W7, Red still has problems; there is that bastion on R7 to get by. By moving in the suggested way White keeps the game in balance; he does not have to be desperate here.

This problem is an excellent lesson in tactics which makes the player think in a logical way. Once again the point is that each position must be considered separately; many look alike, but due to circumstances that are not immediately obvious they must be handled differently.

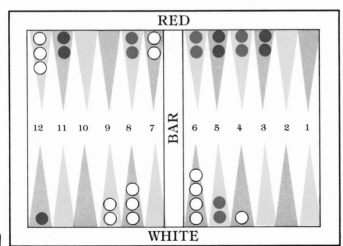

White to
play 6–4.

111

The score was 11–10 in Red's favor in a fifteen-point match, with Red owning the cube. It was the semifinals of an important tournament between two strong young players, one of them — White — already regarded as among the world's best.

The reason for including this position is to show how pressure can affect anyone, even an expert. It is no exaggeration to say that White took at least ten minutes before moving. He couldn't afford to lose a gammon, and this specter was foremost in his mind, naturally inhibiting him from making W5. If Red should get a three — or, even worse, 2–1 or 1–1 — White would be in jeopardy of losing the match in this game, even though Red would need an early six to escape. Therefore White rejected this play, for which he can hardly be blamed, though it looks reasonable from where we all sit with no pressure on us.

How about hitting on W5 and covering W3, leaving a blot on W2? This is more conservative, and unless Red rolls 3–2 or 5–5, White will be in a good position. If he hits on W2, Red would need a three before White entered with a four; and in addition he would have to roll a five or four to escape White's four-point block, and even then White might have two men bearing on the blot. Further, if Red did not roll a four or five immediately, he would have to seriously weaken his board.

But the gammon pressure was so strong that it warped White's judgment, and he rejected this move too. He finally resolved his dilemma by saving his blot on R12 and putting a man in from W7 to W6. This play allowed Red to escape with a five or four, a total of twenty shots, but only fourteen of these carried him past the block on W11. This decision by White shows how tense he was; it was especially wrong not to make W2

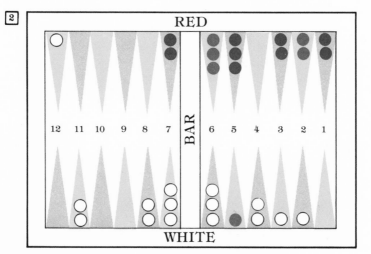

White to
play 2–1.

just in case Red didn't escape. The extra pip gained by putting a man in was not worth it.

There is no intention here of condemning White for his play. Without exception it happens to everyone. Nothing is easier than to be on the sidelines and second-guess a move. What kind of courage does this take? None; you pay nothing if you are wrong. Remember this when you are watching great players in action; once in a while they make the wrong play, which merely proves that they are human too. It is always easier to kibitz any game than it is to play it.

I believe White's best move would have been to hit and cover W3. Under the circumstances pointing on W5 is a little foolhardy, though in a money game it should be seriously considered. White's actual play was not only too conservative in concept, but compounded by not making W2.

112

It looks routine for White to make W4 and secure a prime, but what about those two men on R2? If he doesn't roll a five or six next time, he may have to break his newly won prime immediately. In addition, Red has several chances to make either R7 or R8, which would further restrict White's chances of escape. By far the best play here is to come out with the six to R8 and save the two by moving from W10 to W8. No duplication is involved, but White accomplishes a dual purpose by this move. If hit, he is granted delay and can probably hold his strong front block; if not hit, he has released a valuable man to add to his blocking force.

Here is an example of using your strong forward position to compel your opponent to play men that he would prefer not to move. Wouldn't a prime accomplish this even better? of course, but only if you were sure that you could maintain it. Here you would be in great jeopardy if you made the obvious play to secure the prime because you have no spare men. There is no guarantee—there rarely is—but Red faces a herculean task in releasing his two men on W3 and his one man on W1 if White maintains his present position. Therefore White's priority here is to be sure that he doesn't advance his strong front position too fast. By breaking R2 now he assures this. It may backfire—all close decisions can—but in the long run this tactic will be superior to making W4 and a very shaky prime.

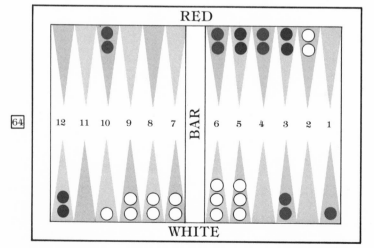

White to
play 6–2.

113

Timing is critical for both sides here. Red is ahead of himself for a back game; moreover, the two and five points are hardly ideal. Still, Red has a valuable man on W5 which he will release on his next turn if he rolls a two, four or five. White is also moving too fast, as evidenced by the extra man on his three point and the blot on his guff. Also, he is stripped in his outer board except for the third man on W8.

Taking all these factors into consideration, what should White do with this 3 – 1? A huge majority of players at all levels except expert would routinely move from W8 to W4. This would be safe for the moment, but with no spare men left in his outer board White will be very vulnerable when he attempts to bring his six outside men safely home. Now is the time to break W11, moving both men from there and leaving a five shot. R5 is open, so if White is hit he still has a good chance, and note what an improvement in his timing he will have effected if not hit. He will have two extra men on W8, plus the blot created on W10—all playable. By the time White has to break R12, Red may have advanced his home board too far, thus lessening White's problems.

Look for opportunities like this, and don't automatically make the safe play and then have to rely on miracles. You have to be prepared to lose occasionally by taking such calculated risks. Many people will try it once, get hit with a five, fail to enter, have Red close his board and then say, "Never again—I'm going to play safe from now on." What they don't realize is that they will lose infinitely more often overall by not boldly accepting these admittedly dangerous chances.

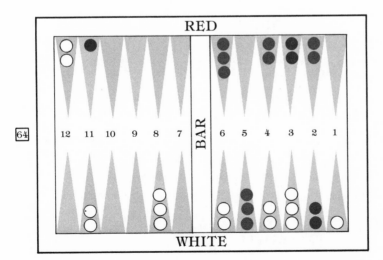

White to play 3 – 1.

114 This is a very tough position, and virtually any move will cause controversy. First, I would not move the blot on W7, but would gamble against Red getting a six or 5 – 1. But should the man on W9 go all the way to W4, or should it stop on W5, allowing the one to be played from R4 to R5? Or perhaps White should break R10, increasing his risk but improving his chances of making W7. If this problem were analyzed by a panel of experts, only one thing is certain: you would not get a unanimous answer.

It is important to realize that if White can make W7 before Red escapes, he does not need the blot on R4 for diversification, for Red will soon have to weaken his outside block. In light of this, I would play the four from R10 to W11, and the one from R4 to R5, even though for the moment it means that I can escape only with fives. If Red gets a one he can hit on R10, but that destroys his block and he has no board. I am convinced that this is the best play. Even if Red gets a six he is not home free, and if he doesn't, White will be more than a 2 – 1 favorite to cover W7. Thereafter he can probably force Red to drop by doubling him.

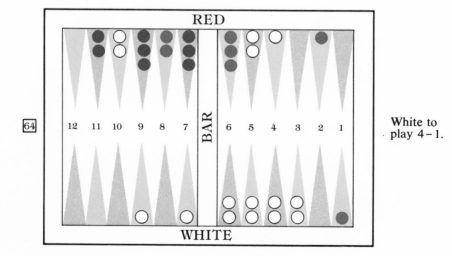

White to
play 4 – 1.

115

Here is a problem on which there are any number of options. To make W7, or perhaps W9, blocking sixes, might be correct. The fourth two would make an anchor on R3. Most players would select either of these plays, both of which are reasonable, but I believe that the greatest priority is to make R5 with three of the twos, and then decide on the fourth. I would make W11, leaving the blot on W7; if not hit, there is an excellent chance it will be covered next time. Besides, if Red chooses to hit with a four he is very vulnerable; he will have lost his anchor and, in addition, must worry about his blot on R11. And if he refuses to hit he is in danger of being confronted with a five-point block.

Never mind about W7 for the moment. Of course you'd like to have it, and probably you can secure it next time. But look at Red's men on R11, R8, and R6, all poised to make R5! Here's an opportunity to make the point before he does. Once again it is simply a matter of priorities. At this juncture, no matter how tidy W7 looks, it has only a fraction of the value of R5.

This play creates a solid defense for White from which he can maneuver handily for the next few rolls. Too many players think of defense as a negative tactic. It simply isn't, and without it your game will always be in jeopardy of collapsing.

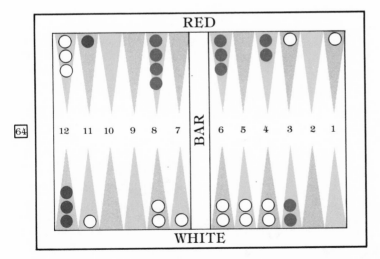

RED

64

12 11 10 9 8 7 BAR 6 5 4 3 2 1

WHITE

White to play 2 – 2.

116

This position is unusual because both sides are stripped in their outer boards and each player has an awkward blot on his one point. It is tempting to hit from W8 and cover W1, but though this play might work (Red could stay out while White built up his board), it just doesn't feel right. If the blot now on W2 should escape, White will face a huge problem in bringing around his men on R3.

Here again White must improvise and go against what he has been taught. To break the midpoint, especially when leaving a blot vulnerable to two shots, seems crazy. But this offers an excellent opportunity for White to play against twos and ones by playing R12 to W7 and W5 to W4. He has a solid anchor on R3, and notice his position if Red fails to roll a two or one. He will be a favorite to cover W4, thereby locking in the man on W2, except for a 6–1. Having secured this point, he can now turn his attention to releasing his back men, and Red will have to exercise care lest White get another man behind his five-point block.

Here is another example of a passive play forcing your opponent to move. If he fails to get a two or a one—and admittedly this is a big gamble—Red will not want to move *any* of his men; since he is not on the bar, however, he will be forced to do so. The bigger the numbers he rolls, the worse his situation will become.

A final consideration: if this play doesn't work and Red hits, no matter what his throw, White is still very much alive.

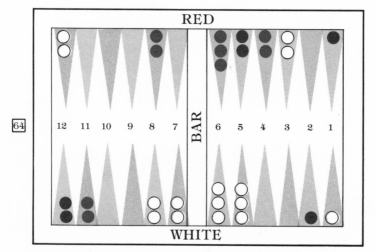

White to
play 6 – 1.

117

This is fairly early, but is still a tough choice. It depends a lot on whom White is playing here. If he is an expert pitted against an average player, he might well start W10 and W3, leaving three blots and attempting to play an all-out back game. He wants to be hit again, and his opponent would probably oblige him. But this is a dangerous approach if Red is experienced. Since he both holds W5 and has a strong defense, he will do all he can to avoid hitting, and White's timing is not good enough to hold his position unless he can delay. Against a good player, White's best play is to move all the way out from R1 and disdain a back game at least for the moment. His strength is R4, without which he would have little chance. But due to this point, even if he should hit on R9 and W11, Red would still have a lot to do before he could double.

Moreover, this latter play doesn't mean that White can't opt for a back game later. If hit now he can easily reestablish a second point in Red's board, and if his timing warrants it by then he could go either way. A position like this shows how intricate the game can become. There is no set plan for either side at this instant, so each player must be able to adjust.

If you are trying to become proficient in backgammon, you could do worse than starting off with this setup. On alternate games change sides. Some interesting end positions are sure to evolve, and you will have many opportunities to improvise, an indispensable requisite if you are to become expert.

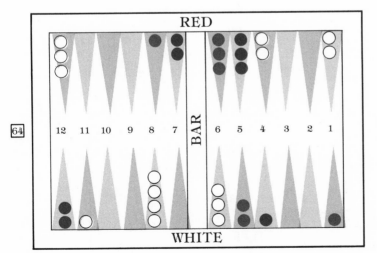

White to Play 5–3.

118

White has a critical decision and many options: (A) W9 to W4 and W6 to W5; (B) W9 to W4 and W8 to W7; (C) W5 to W1, hitting, and R1 to R2; (D) W5 to W1, hitting, and W8 to W7. The process of elimination should be used because each one of the four is reasonable. White should note that Red's timing is far superior; look at how stripped White is at the midpoint. Therefore he must take some kind of action to equalize his position. Consequently (A) must be rejected; it is too passive and allows Red too many opportunities. As for (B), starting W7 is daring and certainly better than (A), but unless White gets a one, he will have to break the midpoint to cover. If White had spare men on R12 and perhaps another builder in his outer board, this play would be best, but since he is so constricted, he should eliminate (B). The choice between (C) and (D) is close, and neither can be criticized.

My slight preference is for (C). It is dangerous to break R1, but Red has no builders in his board, and if White is hit by a one, he is a 3 – 1 favorite to enter and has chances to make R4. It is a good time to activate those back men while Red is on the bar. (D) doesn't seem quite as aggressive, but it is superior to (A) and (B). (Incidentally, I hope nobody considered R1 to R7. This is so foolhardy as to be suicidal. It doesn't attack enough, and exposes White to being blitzed and perhaps gammoned.)

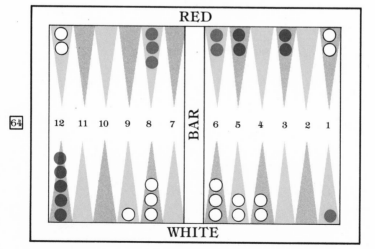

RED

64

| 12 | 11 | 10 | 9 | 8 | 7 | BAR | 6 | 5 | 4 | 3 | 2 | 1 |

WHITE

White to play 5 – 1.

119

White has to be careful to avoid the obvious. Too many would look at this bonanza and quickly make W3 and W8, securing a prime. But what about those two men on R1? They, too, are behind a prime and the timing is such that White is apt to break first. If this happens his whole game will collapse. So he must try to find another way to play this 3 – 1 — which, incidentally, is a great shot for him.

It must be correct to cover W3 with the three, and then White must come up bravely to R2 with the one. He owns the cube, which allows him to make any move he wishes — that is, he can't be doubled and forced to drop. His position is bad, but by playing the one to R2, he gives himself a chance. Now Red may be forced to hit, and if he does, White may stay on the bar and keep his strong front block. There is plenty of risk involved here; Red could roll 6 – 1 and even win a gammon, but not to make the suggested move is to lose by default. Further, White is vulnerable to losing a gammon either way, though admittedly the danger is greater if he splits to R2. Nevertheless, this play is definitely recommended.

Try always to take advantage of any opportunity, expecially when your cause looks hopeless. Until this roll it looked so for White, but now he has a real chance to turn the game around. Don't back off; seize the moment and stand your ground.

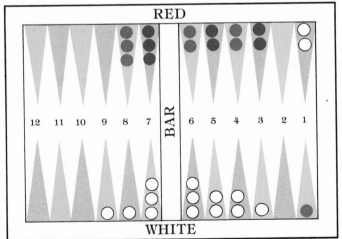

White to play 3 – 1.

RED

12 11 10 9 8 7 BAR 6 5 4 3 2 1

WHITE

120

This position is a treasure trove that runs the gamut of backgammon. There is something for everyone from beginner to expert, and even beyond. I say "beyond" because I believe that under pressure nobody in the world would make the correct play here for the right reason! All of us would misplay it at the table, whether in a tournament or money game. Oddly enough, the rawest beginner might well be the only one to handle it correctly, but for entirely the wrong reason!

Lest the reader feel that I am being too emphatic, let me admit that the first person who played it wrong was this writer in a critical tournament not long ago. Later, analyzing the position at leisure, I became aware that I had made the wrong move.

To cover W1 from W4 with three of the ones is surely correct; no one would argue here. For the fourth one there are three choices: (A) move to R3; (B) move to W5; (C) add a man to W6. Earlier it was stated that there was something in this position for the beginner, and here it is: (A) should be rejected immediately because if you move to R3, only eleven shots free you, whereas if you remain where you are, thirteen allow you to escape. All experts know this reflexively, and comparative newcomers should strive to learn it quickly because it is a common situation.

Hence we are down to two choices: moving to W5, or adding to W6. In all honesty, who would choose (C) between these two? Yet it is far and away the better play! First of all, assuming that Red stays on the bar, there are just as many chances to close W2 next time with two men from R6 as with one each from W7 and W5: double 2's and double 4's versus five and three. In addition, double 2's would play awkwardly if (B) had been chosen, whereas any five can be used to advantage to release White's man on R2 if (C) is played. Furthermore — and this is important

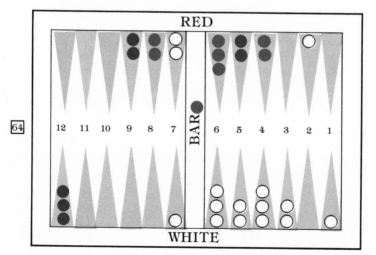

RED

64

12 11 10 9 8 7 BAR 6 5 4 3 2 1

WHITE

White to
play 1 – 1.
Red is
on the bar.

and far from obvious — if White rolls double 6's, 6 – 1 or 6 – 2, look how much better off he is as a result of having played (C)! He cannot move the six and therefore keeps his builders in play. With (B), in each case the six would have had to move to W1 and be out of play forever.

It is true that by having builders on W7 and W5, White would be in a better position to *start* W2, but since he is not going to do so in this position, the only occasion when (B) might be slightly better would be if Red came in immediately. But he is 25 – 11 not to do so, and on the next roll White may be able to split those two men on W6 if he so chooses.

To return to the theory that a beginner might make the correct play for the wrong reason, it would not be surprising for a novice to move to W6 merely for safety's sake. But the safety factor here is irrelevant, because if Red does roll a 5 – 2, he will have turned the game around regardless of White's play, and unless White rolls an immediate five, he will be hard pressed to accept a double.

This position is one of my favorites because there are so many variables. It demonstrates how complicated the game can be when subjected to analysis, and it is frightening to realize the enormous number of subtle (and not so subtle) errors that continue to be made by players of every caliber.

121

This 1 – 1 is one of White's best shots. He enters on R1 and activates those awkward extra men on W3 by making W2, sending Red to the bar. Now for the fourth one. He has two options: (A) W8 to W7; (B) W7 to W6.

This problem was used by a teacher as a way of demonstrating the value of diversifying builders in order to make points. Since (A) would produce two builders and (B) three, (B) was the recommended move. The teacher correctly pointed out that (B) was considerably riskier than (A), allowing four return shots (6 – 1 and 4 – 3) to one (4 – 4) for (A); but that it was worth the gamble. In fact, (B) is exactly three times as likely to cover W4 as (A) is: nine combinations to three! However, in spite of these impressive figures I strongly disagree with the choice of (B).

Here's why. First, White can't spare W7 in case Red enters with a one. Secondly, any two that White rolls is desperately needed to move his back man to R3, so the builder on W6 created by the riskier (B) move is duplicated. Thirdly, though (A) is vulnerable to being destroyed by double 4's, even if (B) is selected, the same roll is probably a winner anyway. (Red would enter on W4 and hit on R1 from R12. If White failed to enter, he couldn't take a double, and even if he rolled a one, he's far from home.) Thus, by playing (B), five shots are bad, and by playing (A) only one is.

I would prefer (A) under all conditions—tournament, chouette, head-to-head—regardless of the score or relative skills of the players. But controversial moves are fun; they add variety and excitement.

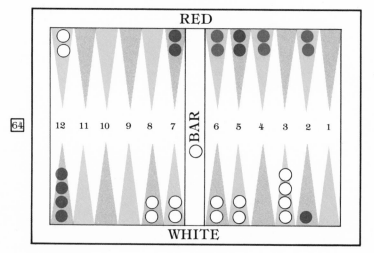

White to play 1 – 1 from the bar.

122

White is faced with a difficult choice. To hit from R5 is dangerous—a possible double gammon shot; that is, if Red stays out he might lose a gammon, and if he enters and hits in return, White could lose the same. Further, if White hits on W5, his only reasonable six is to put a man out of play for good on W3. A third play, which might be best but would be rejected by almost all, would be to save the blots on W9 and on W8. There is no hitting here, but the advantage is that only one man is left open, and since White has Red's five point, he figures to enter long before Red will get all his men around.

The more one studies this position the harder it becomes. There is no real solution. Putting men out of play is always anathema, but so is breaking the anchor. Hitting from R5 would be my choice. At least it is a 17 – 1 chance not to be hit twice, and if Red hits, White may enter with a one or a five. And if by the luck of the gods Red doesn't reenter with a four or five, there is an excellent chance of making W5 and perhaps winning a gammon.

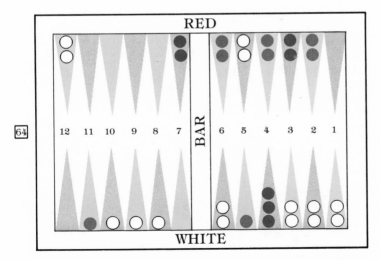

White to play 6 – 3.

123

This problem is a beauty because whatever White does, he is going to run into arguments. He has many options. To hit on W12 and cover W3 would be criminal; indeed, to hit at all is wrong. Undoubtedly most good players and the majority of experts would come out all the way from R2 to R9. In this way they release a man, keep their timing intact, and have a very playable 1 – 3 back game. It's hard to fault this play, since it follows perfectly the concept of back-game strategy. Of course White should welcome either outside blot being hit.

But isn't R1 to R2 and R12 to W7 better? By far the best back-game position is to hold the opponent's two and three points (one and three are the next best). Red has little time left before he has to break his block, and White still has three men in his outer board, plus the blot on R1, which can either be hit or, if not, be used to play any two and subsequent six.

My suggested move is certainly debatable; the first play almost guarantees White's timing, whereas making R2 and starting W7 puts it in a little jeopardy. Nevertheless, I feel strongly about holding the two and three points.

Either way this position cannot really be resolved. It reminds me a little of Debussy's music; often he ends a passage on a seventh chord and leaves you wondering, just as this problem does.

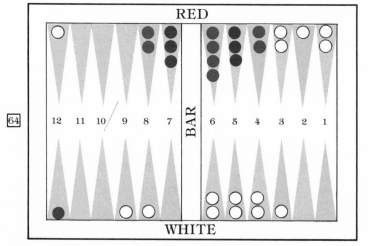

White to play 6 – 1.

124

This is a tricky decision; a lot of angles must be considered. White is in danger of destroying his board, and so would like to be hit again. Therefore what could be better than entering on R2 and hitting on W1? But Red might not roll a one or a two, which would leave those blots badly placed; indeed, he might not even come in. What White has to be sure of *not* doing is making W1, so, if possible, he doesn't even want to start it. Further, he needs a man on R3 so that he can play a five and not have to move off his own six point now or later. It would be nice to enter on R3 and close W2; in this way Red would have to hit to escape. The trouble with this play is that with his men on R11 and R9, Red has a little breathing space; suppose that he does not hit on the next roll and White then gets a six without a five or a four; he will have to go from W7 to W1, which, of course, he doesn't want to do.

It is not easy to solve this problem; perhaps the best move is to enter on R3 and make W5. In this way Red is forced to play whatever he rolls and unless he rolls a six he must hit in order to escape. White will be able to play fives and fours conveniently, and will not be in trouble with a six.

When complicated positions like this arise, it is small wonder that they are mishandled even by experts. There is no actual time pressure as in chess, but the player is under duress, and can't take forever to work out every variation. Still, you can't afford to worry too much about such difficult positions. This one is for experts to chew on—and perhaps disagree with. Which is healthy; backgammon is hardly an exact science, a characteristic that keeps it exciting.

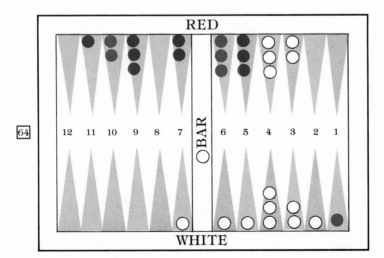

RED

64

12 11 10 9 8 7 BAR 6 5 4 3 2 1

WHITE

White to play 3–2. He is on the bar.

125

This is not an easy problem, but don't look at the suggested play yet. No matter how great or little your experience, take your time and try to consider every angle. As White, what can you do to help your cause here? There are many numbers that would have been better, but on almost every roll one can use this excuse. You can cover W2 and secure a five-point board; you can move to R4, which might make people question your sanity but not your courage; you can move a man in to W5 in a wild attempt to establish a defensive anchor if Red hits the blot on W9.

The strong play is not obvious. It is to hit on W4 with the one and cover W2 with the three, thereby leaving W5 open and a blot on W4. But remember that White has a four-point board and that Red may stay out! Note also that though Red has only a two-point board, he has enormous potential. Somehow he must be prevented from making his bar, which he is a big favorite to do if not harassed. If Red doesn't get a four—and he is 25 – 11 not to—White will be well placed. Moreover, if Red stays on the bar, White will have the pleasant decision of whether to play on for a gammon or double and collect a point, for Red would have to drop with those two vulnerable blots on R10 and R11.

This play is not as radical as it first appears. Always be on the lookout for such maneuvers; they can be vital in turning an impossible position into a winning one. (Incidentally, I would double and grab the point—or welcome a take—if Red stayed out. Red's potential is still formidable, so this is a good example of when not to be greedy.)

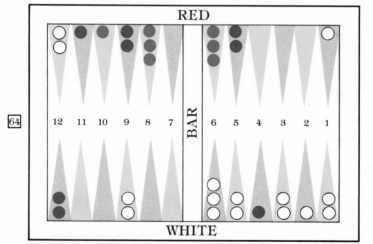

White to
play 3 – 1.

126

With both two points made early, this setup looks contrived, but it came up recently in the semifinals of a consolation tournament match. White took a long while pondering his move, and noticing something from the side lines, I quickly jotted down the position. After a long time White at last shrugged and made the obvious play of moving the two men on R12 to W9 and W8.

Do you see a spectacular alternative which appears far superior to the selected play? How about moving the four from W9 to W5 and the five from W8 to W3? "Has he lost his mind?" some readers may ask—but analyze it. Only ones and threes hit, the very numbers that cover R5. More important, White retains control of R12, his vital outfield post. White's actual play abandons his two back men on R2, and if Red should now make R5, White will have a hard time trying to get them all the way home. In addition, if Red fails to roll a one or a three, White may be able to form a decent board very quickly.

The suggested play seems to me by far White's best bet, but never forget that to sit on the sidelines and analyze disinterestedly is always far easier than making a play under pressure.

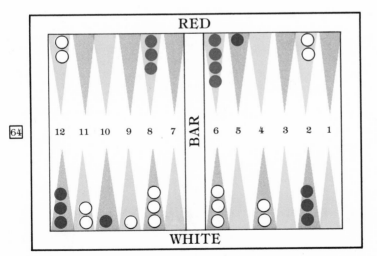

White to
play 5–4.

127

White has much the better game and has rolled the perfect shot. He has several choices. When an opportunity like this comes up, be sure to take your time. What is your priority? Don't you have an excellent chance for a blitz, and if so, how best to exploit it?

As in so many complicated positions, nothing is sure. How about entering on R1 (forced) and making W4, hitting? Or hitting the three blots on R3, W4 and W3? Most people would decide between these two choices, but isn't there yet a better one? White is trying to obliterate his opponent, but if W4 is made, Red will have a chance to make either W1 or W3. Therefore the second option, hitting three men, is better, because unless he gets a double, Red can establish only on W1. But the strongest of all would be to enter on R1, hit on W4 and W3 and then start W7, ignoring the blot on R3 for the moment. Two men are on the bar already, and White wants all the ammunition possible to hit or cover in his board. He is not interested in another irrelevant blot.

Be on the alert for this kind of position, for it occurs frequently and is often misplayed. A good rule to follow is that when attempting a blitz, as soon as you have two enemy men on the bar and still have a number or numbers to play, use the roll to diversify your builders, unless you can hit again *inside* your board.

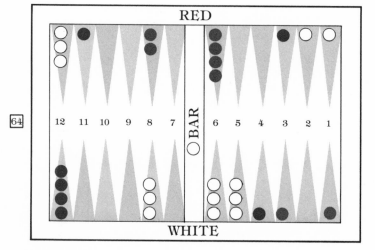

RED

64

12 11 10 9 8 7 BAR 6 5 4 3 2 1

WHITE

White to
play 1–1.
He is on
the bar.

3
THE
END
GAME

Once you are out of the middle game and are ready for the bear-off, you are on firmer ground. There is still much to be done and special handling is required, but most of it can be learned by rote. One basic rule to follow is that if you must leave a blot and have an option on its location, you should expose on the highest possible point in your board. The key is always your *next* roll. If you survive here, the blot farthest up on your home board will be far easier to clear than one lower down. Try not to leave gaps, but if you are forced to do so, also endeavor to leave these as high up in your board as possible.

Remember that both numbers must be played if possible, but that either one may be played first. This rule is misunderstood to an appalling degree, and you should be aware of it to avoid a serious disadvantage.

Bearing off is a science in itself, but again the positions are finite, so they can be mastered. And when you get down to the very end, with only two men left, you must learn by heart the best possible points for them to occupy if there is an option. For instance, if your total remaining count is seven, with two men left, the best points are the five and two, the next best the four and three, and the worst the six and one. There is no logic to this; the dice combinations simply work out this way. Therefore learn all the possible two-man endings and always play them to your advantage. This won't guarantee you a specific game, but in the long run you'll win more often than those who ignore these nuances.

128

White has just doubled, and Red correctly accepts because of his perfect board and the fact that he is well ahead in the race. In fact, this is more of a take than a double.

Except for 1–1 or 2–2 this 2–1 of White's is his best possible shot. He could hit safely on R12, but if Red now rolled a five, White would still have much to do. He could make W5, hitting the blot there and securing a five-point board. This play is not entirely safe because a return 2–2 or 5–2 would hit and probably cost White a gammon. The odds against this are 11–1, so once out of every twelve games on the average White would lose outright with this play. The other choice is perfectly safe for now, but it is going to be difficult for White to make W5 later. Only 2–2, 2–1 and 1–1 would accomplish this because he certainly is not going to slot a man on W5 against a closed board.

On calm analysis there can be little argument about the correct move: White should take the small risk now and make W5. It is vital; if Red should succeed in making it, White would then be only a slight favorite. The reason I stress calm analysis is that though undoubtedly the vast majority of experts would concur, and probably many other players as well, if the position actually arose at a critical moment in a tournament — for example, if the match depended on this game — many of them would make the safe play instead. To have the whole match go down the drain because of a 2–2 or 5–2 would simply be too much for a lot of people. They would instinctively know they were wrong but would still opt for hitting the outside man on R12.

It all depends on the severity of the pressure. To analyze a position when you are not directly involved is a cinch; to execute it correctly under all conditions is what everyone who plays this game should strive for.

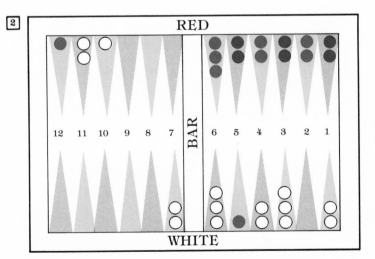

White to play 2–1.

129

This position is almost ludicrous because it seems so easy. But White must be careful. As he prepares to roll, he offers a quick prayer to the backgammon gods that he not get a 6–2, and then panics when it appears. The six comes off, and without thinking the two generally comes off too. Recently I saw this precise play made in a chouette; when asked why, the player answered, "I'm going for the gammon."

Such nonsense is rampant throughout the backgammon world; people simply push men around the board. How much more fun they would have if they applied a modicum of reasoning. For instance, it surely isn't difficult to assume that in this position White will easily win a gammon if not hit. Therefore he should move the two from the five point to the three point, protecting himself from 6–6, 5–5 and 4–4 the next time if Red misses him on the six point. An expert would never take two men off in this situation; it would be routine for him to protect himself.

This problem, easy even for a beginner, is included to emphasize the importance of concentrating all the time, and of never becoming careless under any conditions.

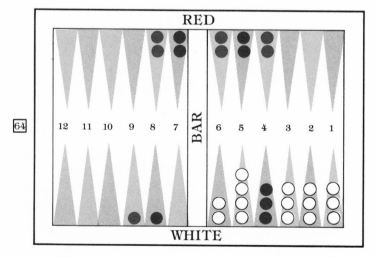

White to
play 6–2.

130

White could routinely play from W9 to W3, be perfectly safe and maintain his five-point block, but he would be stripped on W6 and W7 and therefore vulnerable to leaving shots on his next two turns. Moreover, Red's board is still undeveloped but will probably improve on his next roll. Thus, this is the perfect opportunity to diversify by playing W9 to W4 and W7 to W6. If not hit, White is in great shape to start to bear off. Even if he is hit, R5 is still open, and he will probably have plenty of time to reenter and get around. Also, since Red owns W1 and W2 instead of W2 and W3 or W1 and W3, there are far fewer disaster shots for White if he is hit. Furthermore, if he enters on R1 or R2 and subsequently Red makes R8 or R7, fives and sixes won't hurt White because he can't play them. This is one more example of why the one- and two-point back game is inferior to either the two and three or three and one.

It is true that by maintaining W7 for one more roll Red could not release a back man unless he rolled 6 – 1, but he has a good six which starts his five point. Also, though the suggested play actually is vulnerable to two shots (fives and sixes) realistically it is only susceptible to the six, because if Red elected to hit with a five at the expense of giving up W2, he would be in a precarious gammon position.

You should be aware of this type of play. It occurs frequently, and learning when to use it is an important adjunct to your game.

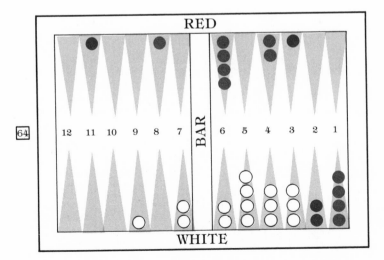

White to
play 5 – 1.

131

Here is a basic bear-off position. What could be simpler? White is well on his way to a gammon, sees no problems ahead and routinely takes two men off from the one and three points, leaving himself even and in no danger. Too many would do this — good players included — but not an expert. What White must do is look ahead and prepare for all possible eventualities. Though in desperate shape, Red will remain a threat as long as he stays on the bar. White wants his opponent to enter; as soon as Red's last man comes in, White's worries are over and he is virtually assured of a gammon. Considering all these angles, instead of taking two men off, White should play two men down from the five point, leaving three men each on W4, W3 and W2. This not only opens W5, facilitating Red's entry, but makes White's next shot safe unless he rolls 6 – 5, 6 – 4 or 5 – 4. This is the risk he takes to solidify his already strong position. Overall he is almost 19 – 1 not to be hit, and even if he is, he still has a chance to recover and escape from Red's home board with a 6 – 1 or 5 – 2. Notice that there would be several awkward shots for White next time if he took two men off — any one, for instance, except double 1's — whereas if he doesn't roll any of the six horror shots he is in as perfect a position as he could ask for without its being a mathematical certainty.

To make the correct play here is a variation of the voluntary-risk principle. It is not easy; you are subject to an avalanche of second guesses if it backfires, but pause and review what your purpose is. Surely it should be to win the game and/or gammon. The latter is assured if you are not hit, so you should do all in your power to avoid this, and, parodoxically, the best way to avoid it is to take a small risk now.

There are many such positions, and though occasionally you will be burned for making the right play, in the long run you will come out ahead.

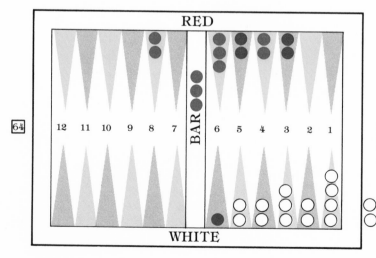

White to play 3 – 1. He has two men off. Red has three men on the bar.

64

132

From an aesthetic viewpoint it would be natural for White to close his board by making W5 and W3, but such a play would be folly. Red might cover W11 on his next shot, and the two men on R12 would be marooned. Even if Red failed to make W11, White's two men on R12 would not be able to get home safely unless he rolled a double very soon, and double 6's would be no good. So instead of being concerned with the beauty of a closed board—which is irrelevant here—White should take a chance now because of Red's superior timing, and bring both men down from R12, leaving Red a three to hit. Since a 2−1 also hits, Red has a total of thirteen shots out of thirty-six. White thus is almost a 9−5 favorite to win because the game is over if he is missed. Why is it over? After all, White may roll double 3's next time and not be able to move his man on W10. If White allowed this to happen he would deserve to lose, because as soon as Red misses, White should double and Red should drop. Of course, this is an obvious action, but it illustrates the necessity of being ever alert to where the cube is and who has access to it. It is surprising how often even experienced players become so absorbed in the flow of the game that they forget the cube. Such lack of concentration is inexcusable.

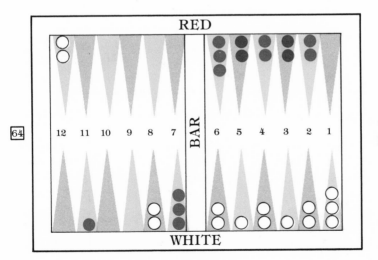

White to play 5−3.

133

Of course White has only one objective: to save a gammon. The principal point here is not to panic. Many players get overwrought in such a position and move their back man as near to home as possible. Others would actually start W1 with the one, and come out to R10. This play would be correct in many situations, but here it proves that White isn't thinking. After Red rolls, White is going to have only one more turn and perhaps not even that if Red gets a double — so he must roll doubles to save a gammon. Thus, preparing his board for a one is meaningless. In positions such as this, take your time and count. After moving the four to R10, look over the board and you will see that with 6 – 6, 5 – 5 and 3 – 3 you will get a man off. Is there any other number? Yes, if you move the blot from W5 to W4, double 4's will also save a gammon. If White is not concentrating, he may think that by transferring the blot on W5 he is killing his chance to get off with double 5's. But the man on R10 bears off with double 5's, so White can afford to immunize himself to double 4's.

Some may belittle such detailed attention to something so apparently picayune, but by playing correctly White reduces the odds against him from 11 – 1 to 8 – 1. Such disciplined thinking is important and separates winners from losers.

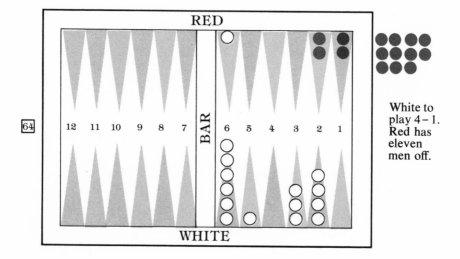

White to play 4 – 1. Red has eleven men off.

64

134

This problem is not difficult if White thinks it through. He has already doubled, and his objective is to get a six and free the back man before he has to break his board. He needs time for this, and his natural inclination is to delay. Therefore many would leave both outside blots where they are and play the two men on W6 to W4 and W2. But by doing this, White is forcing himself to play fives—just what he doesn't want. The position is a paradox, as so much of backgammon is: you seek delay, and to get it you rush men into your board as fast as possible!

To understand this concept is most important because similar situations occur constantly. Players have learned the opposite condition—for example, when you hold your opponent's bar point, and to protect it you keep men in your outer board so that you will have other sixes and not be forced to break. The trouble comes when this principle is applied at the wrong time, as it would be here if the men on W10 and W8 were left outside.

What it comes down to is that you must train yourself to have a grasp of the situation at all times and to realize exactly what your priorities are. The correct play, of course, is to move both outside men to the six point. Now fives don't play, so White has more time to roll that vital six.

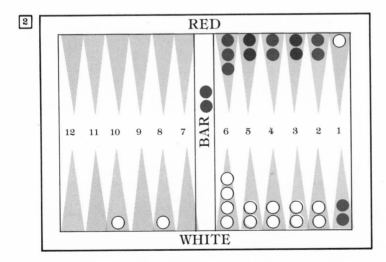

White to play 4-2.

135

Though far ahead, White has an awkward position, especially because of those four men piled up on his three point. Red's board is a threat and White does not want to be hit, so should he play this 6 – 2 safe by moving his extra men to W6 and W3? The answer is no; even though it entails a serious risk, White should reject adding a fifth man to W3 and a fourth to W6. Red's strong board is well on its way to becoming even better, so White must take a stand now to try to diversify his men before it's too late. He should play the six to R2 and two to R7. This makes him vulnerable to a one shot, but aligns his men in a more playable arrangement for the bear-off. It could backfire; Red might hit and make his bar, locking White behind a block and forcing him to destroy his board. But just as calculated risks are taken throughout the middle game, so must they be taken in positions like this when White is almost home free. To give voluntary shots at the eleventh hour rubs the wrong way, but when the alternative is examined there is little choice. If he hits now, Red still needs twos and threes, followed by fives or sixes, to escape, and he also has three blots open in his outer board; therefore, even if hit White is not necessarily lost.

Try to familiarize yourself with this kind of thinking; other problems also stress the same theme. It is important to train yourself when to take such chances and be ready to lose now and then in doing so — all the while being aware that in the long run you will be infinitely better off.

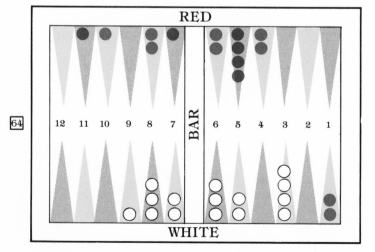

White to play 6 – 2.

136

White's back game is badly timed. His having made W1 and W2 hurts him, and he has no builders. But he has a chance if he will be patient and not hit on R8 from R2. Those nine men on R3 and R4 are extremely awkward, and by moving a man on R2, White would be giving them a chance to bear on the blot left on R2. His best move is to play a man from R5 all the way out to W10, creating a builder for W4. If Red rolls any high number he can't do much, and even such great rolls as 2 – 2, 1 – 1 or 3 – 1 don't solve his problems.

To play back games correctly you must be sure when you hit that you have enough ammunition. In this position White's board is not good enough, and Red wouldn't mind having his own timing helped by being sent back. The odds are extremely high that White will get further shots, and probably there will be double exposures as well. He should bide his time and try to make W4 while Red is entering his home board and necessarily weakening it in the bear-off. Then hitting may well win for him, whereas now it is apt to help his opponent. The negative reasoning that this may be White's only opportunity must be discarded. Too often back games are lost because the player unthinkingly hits at his first opportunity before his defense is secured.

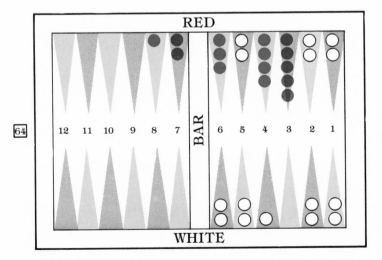

White to play 6 – 4.

137

The first impulse is to play a man from W11 to W6, in hopes of making W2 next time. Red has a strong board which must be respected, and White would be leaving four shots by this play, but if he is hit and fails to enter, Red would be in command. A bolder play is to make W7, leaving blots on W8 and W11. Admittedly this would leave eleven shots, seven more than the other way, yet it is far better. White doesn't want to be hit, but if he is, it is hardly a disaster. How is Red going to extricate his two other back men? White may stay on the bar, but even if he does he will retain his strong front block. Red is favored to break his board long before he escapes from White's clutches.

Of course it is more desirable to give Red only four shots instead of eleven, but the point is that if White is hit on W11 and doesn't come in, he is in such danger that it would be difficult to take a redouble. However, if he is hit on W8, regardless of whether or not he enters right away, he still has much the stronger game.

Here is an example — and there are many — where the number of shots you give your opponent is irrelevant. In this situation you are taking a calculated risk to secure an almost impregnable position — certainly sound tactics.

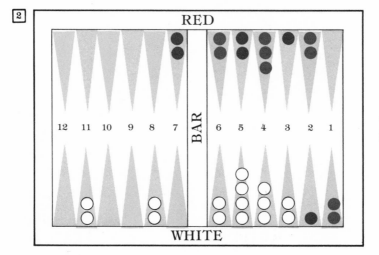

White to play 4–1.

138

This is a welcome one for White, for otherwise he was doomed to lose a gammon. He hits, of course, and now has a three to consider. The only return shot that he is worried about is double 5's, so he should direct his attention to setting up his best defense against it. He should leave the men on R4 and R3, as both will be directly trained on R5, the point on which Red will land if he gets his miracle shot. Therefore twenty shots will hit, but White can do even better if he plays the three from R7 to R10, deliberately leaving a blot so that he will be hit with double 5's. Now twenty-three shots will hit Red. Also, the man on R10 will be in direct range, supported by several combination shots, to hit Red if he should roll 5 – 6 or 5 – 4.

This may seem far-fetched, but why not discipline yourself to extract all the advantage you can out of every position — especially when it costs you nothing? While, of course, White's ultimate objective here is to close W5, he should try to take reasonable precautions against the shot that can destroy him. When he does get his builders into position, he must not be afraid to slot a man; he cannot wait until Red enters and then try to point on him. Red will not stay put on W5 when he enters, for any other number except a one will allow him to escape into White's outer board.

There is a lesson in these positions. Always give yourself the best of it; simply take a little time to count, and learn when and when not to slot a man. To slot is usually correct when a high point is open, as it is here. White could win the game without making W5, but the odds are very much against it. If he can secure it before Red enters, he has made himself a favorite and should be ready to redouble if Red stays out for a roll or two after White begins to bear off.

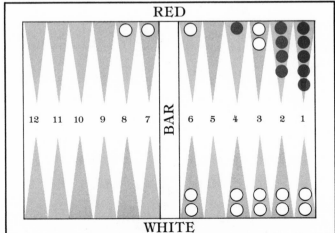

White to play 3 – 1. Red has five men off and it is White's double.

2

139

If White will calmly consider the situation here, he will realize that there really isn't any problem, and will play the six to W4 and hit with the one on W5. Why is it so clear-cut? "Look at Red's board! If he gets a five you're finished," some kibitzer is sure to argue.

But suppose White doesn't hit; how does he stand? He is behind in the race, so Red would be favored. By hitting, White makes himself more than a 25-11 favorite. Why "more than"? Because even if Red gets a five, he doesn't win outright with either 5–1 or 5–5. White will have a chance to roll, and if he enters he will still be in the game. Further, if Red fails to get a five, White can ensure his win by doubling. The fact that the cube is still in the middle, where he has access to it, is a boon, because by doubling now he makes covering irrelevant.

There is a natural aversion to leaving a blot when the opposition has a closed board, but this must not affect White's judgment here. What the position boils down to is that White has a choice of two plays; in one he will be a definite underdog while in the other he will be a pronounced favorite. Under these conditions is it difficult to decide? All that White has to do is to be logical — a pretty good attribute for this game.

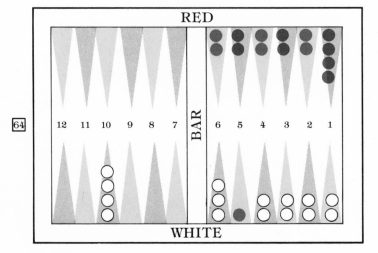

White to
play 6–1.

140

This position is not difficult, but White must be alert. Should he break a point in Red's board, and if so, which? Does it make any difference?

It makes a whale of a difference. White must overcome a natural tendency, which in most other games would be correct, to hold the lowest point for as long as possible, so that your opponent will have a problem getting by you. Here is the exception (in backgammon there is always an exception!). To break R3 would accomplish nothing, because should Red roll a one he can take a man off R1 and not be forced to break R4. But what about twos? If White keeps R2, Red won't be able to play a two and thereby will maintain R4. But look what happens if White breaks R2 and Red rolls 6–2, 5–2, 4–2, 3–2—eight shots which are all disasters. He will have to leave two men open, giving White multiple shots and an excellent chance to turn the game around.

Not to break R2 would be a dreadful blunder, yet when this actual position occurred recently, White correctly broke R2, Red rolled double 2's, annihilating him, then rolled another double and won six points, a triple game. Just to make White's life more galling, an observer pointed out to him that if he hadn't broken R2, Red couldn't have played the double 2's at all and White would still have had a chance to win. Such wisdom offered by kibitzers must be accepted as gracefully as possible, though it is difficult to be stoic under these circumstances.

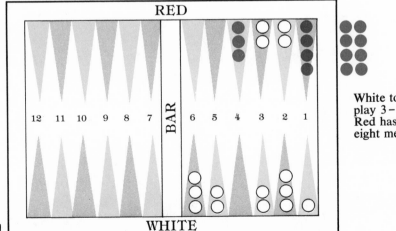

White to play 3 – 1. Red has eight men off.

141

Both sides are awkwardly placed, especially White with those five man piled up on his three point. Red has a four-point board and White has three blots exposed. Of course he hits with the six from R11 to W8, and now must consider his two. The only sensible options are to save his man on W8, moving to W6, which would leave only two blots, both in Red's board, or to hit again on W4, which would place two of Red's men on the bar but would leave a total of four of White's men exposed around the board. Is the choice close? No, it is clear-cut; White should hit on W4. Paradoxically, this is not only White's best chance to take command, but is actually the more conservative choice! If Red fails to roll a four, White has gained a tempo, and if he is hit he still has a chance to secure an anchor in Red's board.

Here is an instance where the inexperienced player might consider it foolhardy to hit twice. Admittedly, bravery is vital if one is to master backgammon, but this position doesn't require it. It takes no courage to play correctly here if you analyze the position. Not to take this opportunity to gain an advantage would show a serious deficiency in strategy. No expert would think twice here, so if you are relatively inexperienced, try to figure out the commonsense reasoning behind this move. Attempt to make the best possible moves for yourself, even though at times they may look wrong or too dangerous. To attain this ability is a vital prerequisite for all aspiring to reach the expert level.

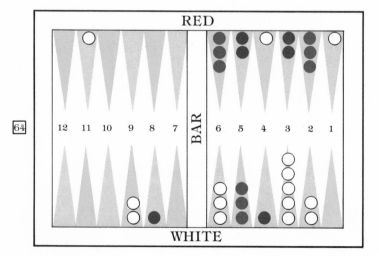

White to
play 6-2.

142

It is White's turn. Should he double, and if so should Red accept? The answer to both questions is yes. Here is a classic example of the 3–1 theory. White is exactly a 2–1 favorite to hit—enough to double—and since Red is less than a 3–1 underdog, he should accept. Too many players would drop here. They see their forlorn blot all alone on W12, vulnerable to a six or one or several combinations, so they concede, because if hit their cause is all but hopeless. Such tactics are costly; these and similar doubles should be accepted. Incidentally, if Red is not hit he should redouble, which White will be hard pressed to take. Red is only even money to get home safely, but even if he fails, White will be a decided underdog to hit—unless, of course, Red rolls 1–1, 6–6 or 6–1.

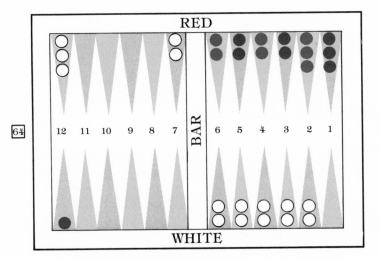

White
to roll.
Should
he double?

143

The natural impulse, hard to resist, is to make W4, securing a prime. But White's objective is not to contain the two Red men on W1; rather, it is to separate them and get them both on the bar. To accomplish this, Red must be given every opportunity to *move*. If W4 is made, Red can only play a one, and it may be a long time before he rolls it. Hence, White must allow Red to play a three as well. Thus White should start both W4 and W2 with his 6–4, leaving blots on W8, W4 and W2. This may seem too wide open, but Red has no defense, and by forcing him to split his anchor with any three or one, White creates an opportunity for himself to put both men on the bar and close his board. If, instead, White allowed Red to hold W1, Red could release at least one man soon after White started to bear off and White would have no more back men to recapture him. What it boils down to is that with two men on the bar against a closed board, Red would be an underdog. With two men on W1 instead of on the bar, Red would be a favorite.

(Incidentally, it might look better and safer to bring two men in from W10, one of them starting W3. But safety is not a factor, and a 6–3 by Red might allow one man to escape for good.)

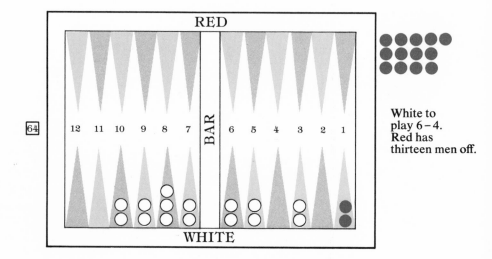

White to play 6–4. Red has thirteen men off.

144

White has no six and must choose between two fours. He could play safe by going to W3 from W7, keeping his prime and perhaps forcing Red to break his board. Or he could move from W8 to W4, giving himself much better diversification but at the same time being vulnerable to a six. Looking at Red's board, the second choice seems too rash. But if this position is analyzed fully, it will be seen that the latter play is clearly correct. Paradoxically, White's good board is not a threat. Let's assume that Red gets a six. If White stays on the bar he will be able to hold his excellent blocking position. Red surely figures to destroy his board before he can release at least two of his other three men. Furthermore, if White does reenter quickly, his men are so arranged that no horror shot confronts him. If White, instead, elects to move conservatively from W7 to W3, he strips himself and becomes vulnerable for the rest of the game. In positions like these always try to give your adversary every chance to destroy himself, so that if ultimately you leave a shot and are hit he will have no board to contain you.

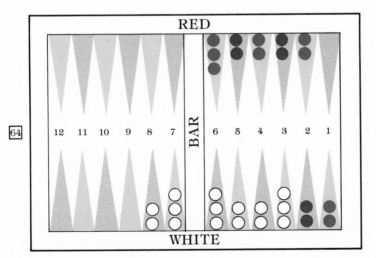

RED

64 12 11 10 9 8 7 BAR 6 5 4 3 2 1

WHITE

White to
play 6–4.

145

White has been trying to bring his two men on W10 to safety for several rolls but has not been able to do so, and now he is at the end of the line. Should he play off W5, leaving himself stripped even further, or risk everything by breaking W10 and bringing one man to W5? If White opens up, which he must do now — he has waited too long already — Red will be a 5-4 underdog to hit.

In situations like this when a blot is left which, if hit, will virtually lose the game, many players feel like sure losers in White's position. Such negative thinking must be avoided, for it will seriously hamper White in making the correct play. If he moves the 3–2 down from the five point, he may be safe for this roll, but on his next turn he *must* roll a double to get those outside men to safety. He could stall if he rolls a few numbers like 5–4, 5–3, 4–3 or 2–1, but eventually these will merely make his position even worse. In fact, if he clears both W6 and W5, he may even have to leave two men open.

When confronted with this 3–2, White's reasoning must be How can I play this to give myself the best chance to win the game? rather than How can I live for one more roll? It takes time to learn to make these plays (to a man, major league baseball managers have never learned this concept, and by intentional walks lose game after game because of it), but as soon as you realize that you are not being foolhardy, or even very brave, but are merely using common sense, you will start to play these positions to your advantage. The mandatory play is to put a man in from W10, leaving a six shot.

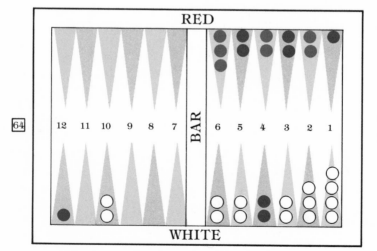

White to play 3–2.

146

Red is presented with an intriguing choice. If he drops, the score will be tied at 14–14; if he takes and loses, he will be behind 16–14, but the Crawford rule doesn't hurt him much because he is at an even number. In other words, he has to win two games in a row, whether or not the Crawford rule is in effect. The enormous difference between being at fourteen instead of thirteen should be noted. It is always best to be at an even number when and if your opponent reaches the so-called Crawford-rule situation, and, of course, you want your opponent to be at an odd number when you reach it.

This position occurred between two experts in a championship tournament a few years ago. After long thought Red dropped. Whether he was correct is still a matter of conjecture, because the decision is moot, and either acceptance or refusal of the double was reasonable. But though admitting that it is a very close thing either way, I opt for the take. Red has six men off, so he can win even if closed out, provided that White doesn't hit his man on R3. Also Red can win the match on this game, which puts great pressure on White; on the other hand, Red can't lose the match immediately, and at worst would be 16–14 behind, needing to win two consecutive games. A sound general principle to follow is "When in doubt, take." Since doubt permeates this position from top to bottom, I would have taken the double.

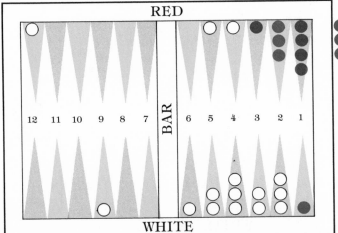

RED

12 11 10 9 8 7 BAR 6 5 4 3 2 1

WHITE

2

17-point match, with Red ahead, 14–12. White owns the cube at 2, and redoubles to 4. Should Red take? He has six men off.

147

This 5–5 is the best possible shot White could have rolled—even better than double 6's—but he has to be careful how he plays it. In games like this, when your defense is gone and you have two or more men to bring around, your chances are poor, especially if your opponent has all his men in play, as is the case here. It would be natural for White to run with both men on R1 and to make R11, hitting. It is safe for the moment, and if he rolls another big double next time he may win a gammon. But it is unrealistic to pin all your hopes on such a long shot. As so often is the case, making R11 is symmetrical, invulnerable and lovely to look at—but only for the moment. The odds are at least 5–1 that White will have to split these two men on the next roll, and then Red will be able to hit them both and probably close White out.

A much better and more far-sighted play is to move one man only, as far as he can go: to W4, hitting twice on R11 and W4. Admittedly, White leaves a blot on W4, but if it is not hit he stands an excellent chance of saving it. He already has seven men off and owns the cube. This, plus the fact that all the rest of his men are down on the one and two points, makes him about even money to win the game. He also has an outside chance of winning a gammon, and of course no risk of losing one. On balance I would pick White to win here if Red does not hit on his next roll.

To play this 5–5 correctly isn't really difficult; all it takes is the ability to think the position through and to play percentage. White must look ahead, but much of the game requires the player to be able to adjust to a particular situation, and not simply push his men around with no thought to the future.

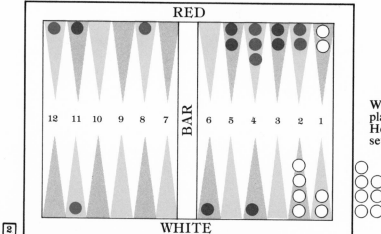

White to play 5–5. He has seven men off.

148

The six is forced; White must play a man to W1 from W7, and now must find a one. Whatever he chooses leaves a 25 – 11 shot, but in this instance the choice could make a big difference. It is natural to break W8 because the blot created will be easier to clear if not hit. However, White should notice how stripped Red's board is and play the one from W4 to W3. If W8 is broken and Red hits with a six, he will maintain his five-point board regardless of his other number. But if W4 is broken and Red hits with a two, he cannot free the same man unless he also rolls a five or a six. In other words, 2 – 2, 3 – 2 and 4 – 2 – a total of five shots – will cause him to break up his board, whereas if he hits with a six on W8, there are no shots which will make him break.

A further reason to leave the two shot is that even if Red hits and escapes with a 2 – 5 or 2 – 6 he still has another man back which needs a two followed by a five or six. If Red's three extra men on R2 were in his outer board so that there was no chance of his inner board collapsing, then White should open the blot on W8, which leaves him in a much better position if he is not hit.

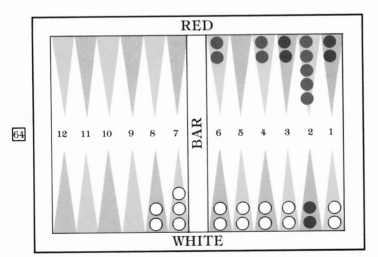

White to play 6-1.

149

This problem is similar to No. 160 in concept. All White has to do here is to keep his wits about him and count. He has two choices; (A) take the six off and move down to W1, breaking W4; (B) hit on W3 with the three (remember that he may play either number first, as long as he plays both) and take the six off the four point, leaving two blots.

White's reasoning should go as follows: I own the cube, and no matter how I play this 6–3 I get a man off, so there's no danger of losing a gammon. If I am hit, I am almost a sure loser because Red has a prime, which makes him a prohibitive favorite. Therefore I'd better leave the fewest shots possible.

When White considers his predicament in this manner, he is well on his way to the right play. It is probably a surprise to many to learn that (B) is the better choice here. At first it looks foolish to leave two blots, whereas (A) leaves only one. But White would be vulnerable to twenty-six shots with (A), and to only twenty-one with (B). The risk of having two men back might deter many players, and they wouldn't bother to ponder further. But since White is all but beaten if hit even once, the extra man is for all practical purposes irrelevant.

This is one more example of how the right play looks wrong. You must train yourself to select the correct move even if at first glance it seems illogical.

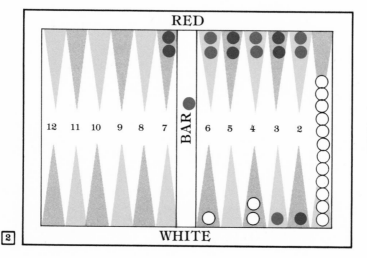

White to
play 6–3.
Red is
on the bar.

2

150

Here again this problem deals with priorities — but then there is hardly a game in which somewhere along the way they don't play a major part. White has been lucky to hit his opponent after Red has removed twelve men. He has almost surely saved the gammon, and now must set his sights on winning. Since Red has those two blots on R1 and R2, White can still do so, but he must hit at least one of them; he can't afford to let Red make R1. How best to accomplish this? White should not get careless here and make W9, securing a prime. His priority is quite different. He must hit on W1 from W8, because by doing so he changes 6-1, 5-1 and 4-1 into disaster shots for Red instead of winners. There is nothing that White can do about 3-1, 2-1 and 1-1, but by moving correctly here White deprives Red of over half of these instead of giving him eleven good ones. Note also that if Red enters with 6-3, 5-3 or 6-2, he must hit White and place the two blots in his home board under attack. White has reduced Red's winning numbers to five, so Red is over 6-1 not to solve his problem, at least on this roll.

Here is one more example of the necessity of being aware of what is most important in any given position. In the vast majority of games you should concentrate on securing a prime; here it is practically irrelevant.

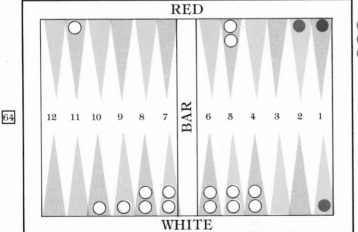

White to play 5-2. Red has twelve men off.

151

White is barreling toward a gammon, but in his haste he should be careful. This 3–1 leaves him vulnerable to any two different high numbers next time because now he must take a man from W4 to W1. Certainly, he isn't going to leave a shot voluntarily, so he won't hit with the one. The routine play is to take a man off from W4, not hitting. The blot on W1 is in no danger, so how can this play be wrong? Further, it leaves White with an even number of remaining men.

But White must look deeper. What if he gets two big numbers next time and Red hits him on W4; does White want to have that vulnerable blot on W1? If hit on W3 he will have seven or eight men off, and stands a good chance even if Red closes his board, but if he is hit again on W1 he is finished. Therefore his best play here is to reinforce W1, leaving three men each on W4, W2 and W1, and not bear any man off. His gammon is virtually assured if not hit, so carelessly taking a man off here is a nullo play; that is, it can't gain anything, and it may lose everything.

There are many other instances of nullo plays; try never to be guilty of them. It is acceptable to take the most daring risks imaginable, provided they produce commensurate rewards if successful, but never make a play that can only lose.

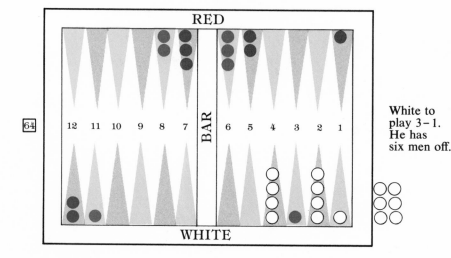

White to play 3–1. He has six men off.

152

White doesn't have to count pips in this position. Thanks to the forward men in his board more than the actual count, Red is well ahead in a race. Therefore White was poised to hit with any odd number, whether or not it meant leaving two blots. But he rolled 6–2, and now must make the best of it. Either W10 or W8 has to be broken, and since he must do everything possible to contain Red, he should hang on to W10, blocking fives. Hence he goes from W8 to W2 with the six. Now it is almost a reflex action to play W8 to W6, but if White takes his time he will realize that this blot may hinder Red if left on W8. For instance, suppose Red rolled 3–3, 5–3, 5–5, 3–2, 2–1 or 1–1 and the blot wasn't there. He would escape with his remaining back man with either of the first two, and be in much less danger of being hit if he rolled any of the last four. If he has to hit on the way, he will give White two shots on R2 and R3, and if he elects to remain on W5 or move to W7 with 2–1 or 3–2, the blot on W8 will be another builder with which to hit him. His best two is to make W1, not W2; it keeps his builder diversification more flexible.

Becoming this analytical takes a great deal of concentration, but if you want to become expert these nuances add up, and the more you are aware of them the better off you will be.

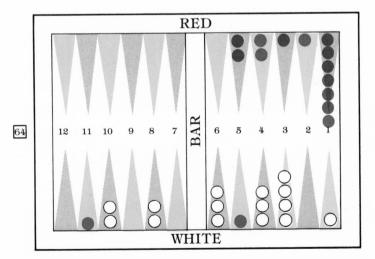

RED

BAR

64

12 11 10 9 8 7 6 5 4 3 2 1

WHITE

White to play 6–2.

153

To begin with, this is more of a take than a double. There are thirty shots that hit, so White is a 5–1 favorite to do so. But aside from the remote possibility of missing, the danger is that White will hit only one man, and that Red will be able to save the other. In which case, with his fractured board, White will be in for a rough time, especially because his opponent owns the cube. If White's board were closed, or even if he didn't have an extra man on W3, I would unhesitatingly double here, and only a desperado would take it. Though it is true that White could conceivably lose a gammon here if he misses, Red could also lose one if both his men are picked up.

The position being what it is, however, my gut feeling is not to double; I would roll and see what happens. Still, no fault can be found with anyone who chooses to double. So much in backgammon is debatable. Remember this, especially in chouettes when you are part of the team against the box. Never be adamant, no matter what the other man's move. He may be wrong, but even so, his play, though inferior in theory, may turn out to be a winner. There is no game known to man where the "wrong" play so often turns out to be right. Therefore let your partner have his way and pray that he lucks out; it makes for a much more pleasant atmosphere.

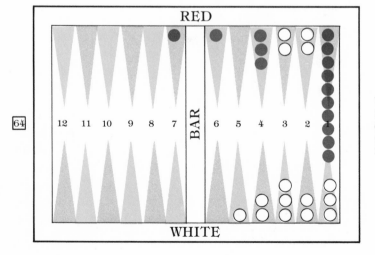

White to roll. Should he double? (Red has ten men on R1.)

154

Positions like this occur extremely rarely, but it is good to have your wits about you when they do. There is hardly a player—beginner, intermediate or expert—who would not routinely take off a man from W2 and play the one safe to W1, leaving five men there. This virtually assures his gammon, which, at worst, ties the match and gives him an outside chance to win a triple. It is pretty tough to fault such a play, but once again let's assume that you are new at the game and pitted against an expert. If you settle for 19–19, he is still a favorite. Do you see the possibilities? What if you take two men off? He has two on the bar, and if he doesn't roll a double or a two you have a chance to win the match right now!

When making a play like this, you must always consider the down side. If you are hit, you are still a favorite because you will have eleven men off, and even if he closes his board you should win two points and be behind 19–17. The point is that you should at least *consider* this move, even if eventually you decide against it. Remember that Red is a 25–11 underdog to hit the two, and that if he misses, you will of course have a gammon. But if he should roll a one and no two, you are heavily favored to win the match in the next two rolls.

To make such a play takes courage and imagination. But if you ever get the opportunity, gird up your loins and do it; I can guarantee that your opponent will hate having to roll that two to save himself.

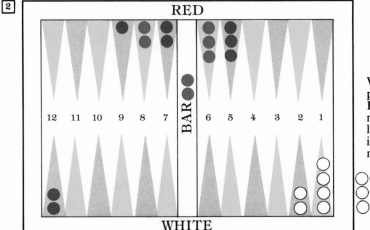

White to play 6–1. Red has two men up and leads 19–15 in a 21-point match.

155

By playing correctly here, White is going to lose on the average once out of eighteen games, but if he opts for the safe move he will wind up losing far more often in the long run, even though he cannot be hit on Red's next roll.

The right play is to put the five in from W8 to W3, and to split from W5 to W4 with the one, creating a diversification of builders. Kibitzers will bombard you with reasons for not having left that blot, especially if Red produces a 6 – 1 to win the game, but backgammon is made up of calculated risks, some relatively unimportant and some so vital that the outcome of the game depends on their success. Don't shy away; make the play that gives you your best chance to win the game, not merely the one that will get you by until the next roll.

Notice how much more balanced and fluid Red's position is if he takes this 17 – 1 chance. He will be in much better shape to be able to play safe or to point on Red next time. Note also the power of Red's position. His board guarantees a win if he hits, because White could not take a re-double.

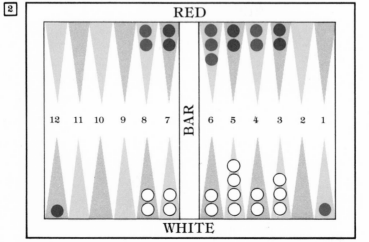

White to play 5 – 1.

156

White has already doubled and Red wishes he had dropped, for there is strong potential for a gammon, and White should focus his attack on this objective. The 2−1 is not good for him. What he's interested in is the blot on W2, not the one on R4: he wants to erase Red from his home board. He has already secured a full prime so that Red can't escape from W2.

What should White do? Since Red already has a man on the bar, he can afford a most unusual play. He should abandon his prime temporarily in an all-out attempt to keep Red from establishing a point in White's board. Awkward as it appears, what White should do is hit on W2 from W4, and then make W1! This is slightly better than hitting from W3 and making W1, but both plays are far superior to woodenly hitting on R4 and playing the two to W4. Too many players would do this, feeling secure because of their prime. What they must realize is that if Red should now roll a two − any two − he will pose a threat until the very end, by which time he will have a fine board. White could well leave a shot later which might cost him the game.

By making the suggested play, White leaves himself open to the disaster shots of 4−4 and 2−2, but the odds are 17−1 against Red rolling either. However, if the blot on W2 is left alone, the odds are only 2−1 against Red making this point on his next roll (any 2, plus double 1's). White should make the suggested play in all circumstances. Even if a gammon is not relevant, it is still better to try to close Red out rather than to let him establish on W2.

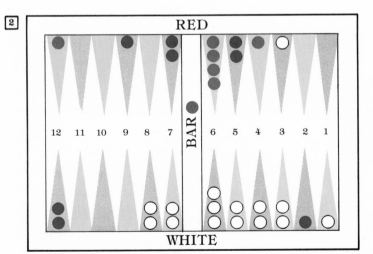

RED

12 11 10 9 8 7 BAR 6 5 4 3 2 1

WHITE

White to play 2−1. Red is on the bar.

157

White has already doubled, and now has three choices: (A) he can play safe by putting two more men on his one point; (B) he can bear one man all the way in to his six point, leaving a direct three shot; (C) he can play both men from R10, leaving himself vulnerable to an eight or nine.

A large part of backgammon is made up of such decisions. There is merit in all three choices. To bury two builders is distasteful, but Red may wish on his next turn to move his man on W12, thus partially freeing White's men on R10. To risk being hit by a three — (B) — gives Red fourteen shots, making White about an 8 – 5 favorite, whereas (C) would allow only eight shots, making White a 3½ – 1 favorite to survive. But the drawback to (C) is that *two* men would be vulnerable, and if either was hit and White failed to roll a six immediately, he could lose a gammon. Certainly he would have to drop if doubled.

Which of the three is best? There is no sure answer, but the longer one plays, the more one tends to reject (A). This kind of cowardice has a way of backfiring, though once in a while it pays off, as even the weakest plays can. The fact that R6 is open tips the scales in favor of (B). At least only one man can be hit, since all others will be safely home, and even if he is picked up, White has several chances to roll a six and still win.

Learn to discard such plays as (A); in the long run they will come back to haunt you and prove to be suicidal.

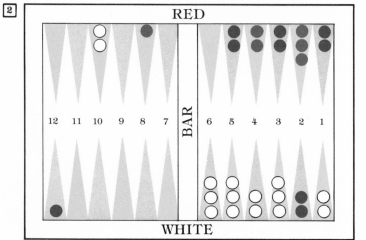

RED

12 11 10 9 8 7 BAR 6 5 4 3 2 1

WHITE

White to play 5 – 4.

158

This interesting position occurred in a chouette recently. The game was generally of a high standard, though you may question this when you compare the actual play that was made (W6 to W3 and R11 to W10) with the less obvious but undoubtedly correct one. Can anyone but an expert be criticized here if he immediately makes W3 with the three and then looks around for a four? The vast majority of players would do this without thinking. But lack of thought is responsible for most bad play. Doesn't White have to get a second and/or third man back to have any reasonable chance in this game? Certainly, but how best to accomplish this? Of course he wants Red to have to split his two men on R2, and to do this, Red must roll a one. But if W3 is made, W2 is left vacant, and if Red rolls a one, he simply moves to W2 and keeps his men on R2 intact. Therefore, even though it looks awkward and would be incorrect in most other situations, the right play is to make W2 with this 4 – 3, leaving the blot on W3. Now *any* one except double ones — against which there is no defense — will destroy Red; he will be forced to break his point and leave three men open around the board. Admittedly, this play risks a 5 – 2 by Red, but even this doesn't guarantee a win, and to give a 17 – 1 shot in exchange for a 13 – 5 shot (ten ones) must be sound.

Should White redouble immediately if Red gets a one? In most cases, yes, but in all money games Red should also take, because if White fails to roll a one or a two, Red may be able to make R1 and again become a prohibitive favorite.

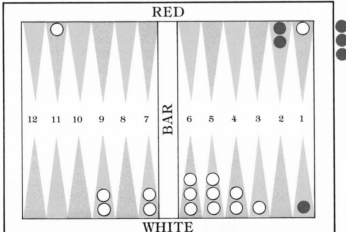

RED

12 11 10 9 8 7 BAR 6 5 4 3 2 1

WHITE

White to play 4 – 3. Red has twelve men off.

2

159

Settlements are not as frequent as they once were, mostly because they are forbidden in tournaments. Such a rule makes sense because if allowed they cause mammoth delays. It is a shame, because settling is an art involving judgment, psychology and skill. But in money games there is still plenty of bargaining, and when you hear two people haggling back and forth you might think you were in a Baghdad bazaar.

This position came up in a friendly but high-stake game between experts. White owned the cube at eight, but before he rolled, Red suggested that they settle. Of course each wanted the other to make an offer, the usual ploy, and there was much stalling. Finally White declared that he would take one and a half points, observing that he would hit Red with nineteen shots. But Red refused, saying that he considered himself a slight favorite, since he was ahead in the race; further, the blot on W1 might need a four to cover, the same direct number that White needed to hit. Hence, no agreement was reached, and White proceeded to roll 4−3, as perfect a shot as he could want. He hit and covered, Red failed to enter, White redoubled and Red dropped.

Both players were experts, but I agree with White that he was entitled to some payment. The reason? Because he owned the cube, a most pertinent factor here. Even if White missed, Red, not being able to redouble, could roll 1−1, 2−2, 4−4, 3−1 or 2−1 and still be in jeopardy. Also, White could conceivably win in a race. If Red had owned the cube, even White's tremendous 4−3 shot wouldn't have won outright for him because Red still would have an opportunity to roll 2−5 or 2−6 and perhaps escape. Once again this position emphasizes the enormous value of owning the cube. Indeed, I believe that I would take *either side* of this proposition, providing that I had the doubler; that's how strong a weapon it is.

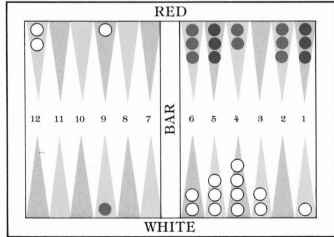

White's turn
to roll.
What is
the right
settlement?

One final but very important point: never be afraid of a game in which settlements are employed. If you feel uncomfortable or unsure of what to ask or give, you can simply refuse all offers and never make any yourself. In this way you are no worse than even, and in some cases you have actually gained an intangible edge by disconcerting those opponents who go into a smooth sales pitch, only to have you firmly turn them down.

160

Here is an intriguing problem that came up in a European tournament three years ago. Of course the man on R8 has to be moved six pips, but there are several choices for the one. No matter how long they have played the game, most people will look at this bizarre layout, then save the man on W4 and play the forced six. Such a move would probably be natural to over 95 percent of the population, especially under pressure. Even when presented as an interesting position, where there is time to ponder it, players usually wind up saving the blot on W4.

But in this situation backgammon once again shows its many facets. As is so often the case, the natural play must be discarded. If he thinks the situation through, White will begin by realizing that if he is hit he is finished (Red has the cube), so he must try to give the least number of shots. If White saves the blot on W4, he will leave twenty-eight shots, but if, instead, he hits another man on W2, leaving blots on W4 and W2, and two of Red's men on the bar, he leaves only twenty-one shots! To put it statistically: by saving the blot you make your opponent a $3\frac{1}{2}-1$ favorite to hit, but if you hit him he is only a $7-5$ favorite. There can hardly be any doubt which is the correct play.

This game was for the match between two experts, and a gammon was irrelevant. Besides, White had three men off and couldn't lose one in any case, so his wide-open play could cost him no more than two points. White made the correct move after long thought. Red missed, and White went on to win. As soon as the match was over he was deluged by howling kibitzers: How could he have made such a ridiculous move when the game was so important? Filled with euphoria, he politely began to explain, yet several in the group simply could not grasp his reasoning. One ob-

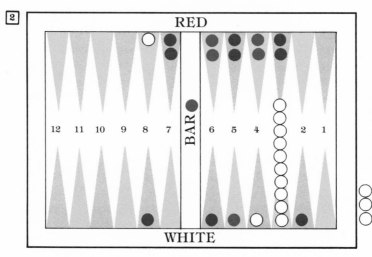

White to
play 6 – 1.
White has three
men off,
and Red
is on the bar.

server said angrily, "Well, I know you're supposed to be a great player, but I don't care what anybody says; leaving two men exposed when you don't have to in a nonexistent board . . ."

Walking by, another world-class player heard the kibitzer's tirade and grasped the position quickly. The two experts shrugged their shoulders and smiled at each other.

161

Red's timing is bad but he still presents a threat. Both sides want to delay. This position has many ramifications and the correct play is so difficult that it probably would be overlooked by everyone, including experts, in the heat of battle. What White wants is to force Red to move a four inside his board off his five point. Fives and sixes won't hurt him. But if White moves his blot on W8 to W2, which most would do, he allows Red to exit with a four, thus preserving his shaky board. So White plays the one from W9 to W8, blocking fours. By doing this, he leaves an awkward five. His only sensible solution is to go from W10 to W5, leaving two blots vulnerable to a five or six. If Red gets a five or six, he automatically releases a man from W3 or W4 and White welcomes the delay, especially because Red's six point is open. Further, if Red does not get a five or a six (he is only a 5–4 favorite to do so), he may have to start destroying his board. If he is forced to make R1, those men are out of play for good. Remember that every one of the twenty-four points on the board can be made, broken and remade except this single one, the dreaded "guff," as it is called, because once made there is no way to break it before the bear-off.

This problem was mishandled by a renowned player in an important tournament, but to analyze every aspect of it under pressure is most difficult. After the match was over, the position was analyzed and discussed at length. When all the pros and cons of the different moves were examined, in the consensus of expert opinion the suggested play was best.

There is no end to the subtleties inherent in backgammon. Sometimes it is next to impossible to spot the correct play immediately because there are so many angles to consider. But in most cases a player will be able to solve a large portion of them if he can follow a simple chain of priorities leading to the main theme.

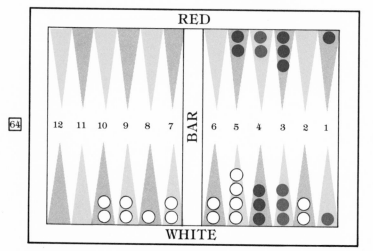

White to play 5–1.

162

Like almost all positions, this one has more to it than at first seems obvious. Red is far ahead in a race, so White wants to contain him. But if he hits, he can't cover both blots, and it takes a strong constitution to leave a man open in light of Red's closed board. White must weigh his options. If he hits and closes W2, he is a 25-11 favorite not to be hit, but he also must be aware that he is a 3½-1 favorite not to be beaten outright if Red rolls a four. Why? Because 4-2 and 4-4 leave White a blot of Red's to be hit on his return shot. Moreover, by hitting, White blocks *all* doubles by Red (double 4's being partially blocked), and Red can roll only one number (not counting fours) which will free him completely (6-5). Hence, hitting is much less dangerous than it looks.

If you should ask most players at random what they estimate Red's chances of clearing his blot on W4 to be, they would hesitate, then start to count the rolls. But if you made it simpler — "Never mind the exact odds; is Red a favorite to get out or not?" — I'll wager the majority would answer, "Of course he's favorite, but I don't know by how much." In point of fact, if Red were to roll from where he stands on W4 against the points White has on W6, W8 and W10, he is a 7-5 underdog to escape!

So two facts have emerged: the danger of hitting is comparatively small, but also Red is far from home free if not hit. What, then, is the right play? I would hit and cover W2. Only ten shots win outright: 6-5 and all fours except 4-4 and 4-2. By not hitting, fifteen shots free Red, and though White will still have a mathematical chance, he can't accept a double unless he rolls a large double immediately after Red's escape.

There's a lot of detail here, but it is worth analyzing because it shows how complicated this game can be if you consider it from all angles.

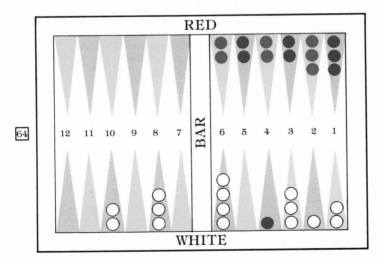

White to play 2-1.

163

There are two schools here. By not hitting on W2 and moving his blot from R11 to W10, White forces Red to play. Unless Red rolls a three, he will almost certainly have to break his board some more, just what White wants. But a 6-3, 5-3 and perhaps a 4-3, a total of six shots, will win for Red. Hence, the alternative choice of hitting on W2 and making W5 at the expense of W7 is probably best. Even if Red now rolls a two he must also get a five to escape. Further, 4-2 and 3-2 are very bad for him. White is gambling against the miracle 5-2, which might cost him a gammon, but considering all the ramifications, it seems best for him to risk it.

Always be alert for situations where you want to force your opponent to play and ruin his position. In such cases you should refrain from hitting, lest he fail to enter and thereby keep his board. Here these conditions exist, yet because of other factors they must be ignored. It is not worth allowing Red six possible winning shots in order to have him break if he fails to get a three. A much stronger play is to gamble against the 5-2, the only sure winner for Red, because even if he gets a two he may have to break his board before he rolls a five, and meanwhile White has a chance to enter immediately on Red's six point.

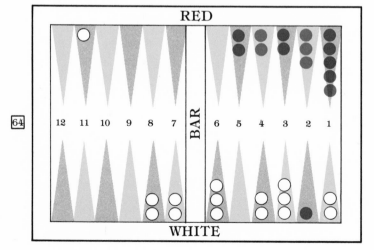

RED

64

12 11 10 9 8 7 BAR 6 5 4 3 2 1

WHITE

White to
play 1-1.

164

Here is a marvelous position which occurred in a chouette — meaning that there were arguments galore about how to handle it. White has been doubled; he has an opportunity to win if he can pick up another man, but at the same time he must be concerned about losing a gammon, or even a backgammon. What should he do?

In a money game it seems to me that the solution is clear-cut: White should go for the win. He can do this handily and at the same time give himself excellent insurance by playing the five to R12 and the one to R11. He thus guarantees himself a double shot if Red gets a six, no matter what the other number is. The natural play here is to hit on W1 with the one, but this would diminish White's chances of picking up another man. He wants Red to break R2, but this can be accomplished only if Red rolls a one. There is nothing that White can do about double 1's, but unless Red rolls a six, he will have to break R2 with all other ones — a total of eight shots. However, if White hits Red on W1, there is no number which will force Red to break. Therefore by far White's best chance is to block Red's double 6's and not hit, thus forcing his opponent to play a one from R2 to R1.

By and large in a tournament, the same play should be made, though in isolated cases it might be handled differently. For instance, if White was an expert and was leading a novice 15–11 with the cube at four in a 19-point match, it would be reasonable to hit. To risk losing eight points and the match if Red escapes is too much of a chance. Also, if White closes Red out even without getting another man, he still has an outside chance of winning the game and the match. Also, even if Red does win, White, as an expert, is still a favorite at 15 all. But in the vast majority of cases White should not hit here with the one.

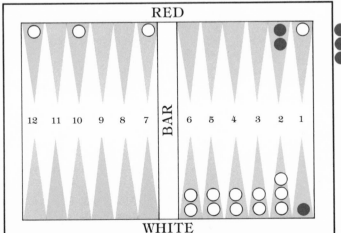

White to play 5–1. Red has twelve men off.

165

This position is tough. There are so many questions and answers. First of all, not everyone would double; White is almost an 8–5 underdog to hit, and only a 5–4 favorite to enter. But his reward if he does hit is an almost sure gammon. Many factors should enter into both sides' decisions. In a tournament you should double if you are less experienced than your expert opponent. Such a play creates leverage. Moreover, if White fails to come in and Red immediately redoubles to four, White should take. Though Red is a 2–1 favorite to cover R1, R5 is open, and White has a perfect board. If Red rolls one of the twelve shots that don't cover R1, White owns the cube at four, with a chance to win eight! (Also if a gammon were relevant in a tournament—at 11 all in a fifteen-point match, for instance—from Red's viewpoint this is a murderous take because he can too easily lose the whole match on one roll. Realizing this, White should double; most opponents would drop, and White will thereby win a valuable point by default.)

Situations like this should be exploited even if they backfire; they offer by far your best chance to beat any expert. Try to load as much as possible on one all-or-nothing shot. Of course if you are Red and are doubled by a more experienced White, you should take with glee and redouble immediately if he doesn't enter. This is the advantage the neophyte has, if only he will realize it. The true expert will not double his less knowledgeable opponent here unless he is convinced that he will drop.

Herein lies much of the skill of tournament play. When you see an expert double and induce a drop in this position you should silently congratulate him. He took a big gamble and read his man correctly. Don't point out later how dangerous it was; he knows this.

In money games, a sound policy for White might be to double going

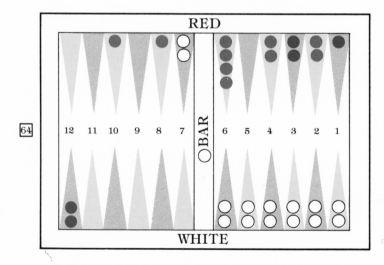

White is on the bar. Should be double, and should Red take?

for the gammon, but to be prepared to drop immediately if he doesn't roll a five or a one. White is risking two to win a likely four, with the odds only about 8 – 5 against him.

This problem illustrates a few of the subtleties that have to be examined when the doubler is the focus of the action. There is hardly a position in backgammon where one can look at an isolated alignment and give a sensible answer without knowing which side has the cube.

166

White has been doubled. He is in bad shape, but there is a chance he will get a shot, and if he hits he could still win. In this position he must be aware of two facts. His first priority should be to save a gammon if possible. Secondly, he should close his board in preparation for a potential shot. But these two priorities have to be attended to in that order, not the reverse. Therefore his move should be W12 to W6 and W11 to W6, putting two men in and leaving the blot on W5 uncovered. If he makes the more obvious and natural play of securing W5, he will leave a man outside on W7, and this minuscule difference could cost him a gammon if he doesn't get a shot at Red or if he misses hitting.

Often in backgammon it is necessary to discipline oneself to follow priorities in order of their importance. Here White may never even get a shot, and if so, will of course need to utilize every pip and crossover* to save a gammon. Admittedly, there is a risk involved; if on his next turn Red rolls any of his twelve bad numbers, leaves a shot, White hits, and now Red comes in immediately with a five, White will of course be sorry that he didn't cover when he could have. But the odds against this sequence occurring are more than 30−1, so White is correct in saving every pip he can right now, starting with this 6−5.

*There are four quadrants on a backgammon board, each containing six points, and a crossover is effected when a man is moved from one quadrant to the next. As many crossovers as possible should be played when there is a race to your home board, particularly when you are trying to avoid losing a gammon.

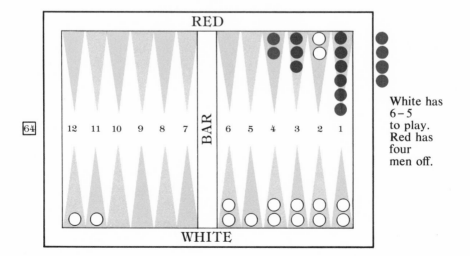

White has 6−5 to play. Red has four men off.

167

Here is a position which forces the player to improvise. White wants to contain Red on W1, but has no builders to hit him. Red has no board, but he does have an avalanche of men ready to hit and make R5. White cannot play safe no matter what he does; his least exposure would be to move his blot on R12 to R10, leaving him vulnerable to a three. But since he has a board and Red doesn't, White should make the extremely unorthodox play here of hitting on W1 from W2 with the one, and then covering R12 with the two.

To be sure, this play leaves two blots in White's board in addition to the man exposed on R5. But if White can immobilize Red for this one roll—and his only chance to do so is to hit—he will be in a great position. He will have Red's blot on W7 to hit, and can probably make him drop if doubled, for it would be a foolhardy take.

If White elects not to hit, there are too many good rolls available to Red. A six will get him out of White's board and makes W7, and many other numbers make R5, pointing on White. It is a dangerous play, of course, but at least it limits Red to twos and ones, rather than allowing him to use almost every number to his advantage.

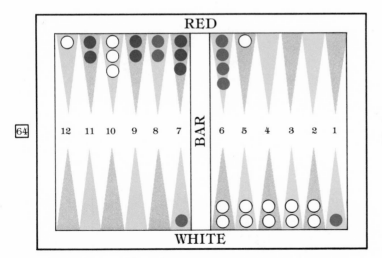

White to
play 2 – 1.

168

This position arose in a recent tournament on the West Coast. A gammon for White was irrelevant because he was one point from victory and it was a Crawford-rule tournament. How would you play this 4–3? White was an expert, and many players would agree that he made the correct move in putting two men in from W8. After the match, which White won, I suggested to another player that hitting from W9 would have been superior, and he confessed that he had never even considered the play. I was surprised because to me it clearly seems best even though a gammon is not involved. If Red succeeds in establishing on W2, he will be a threat until the end, so while he has a prime White should take this opportunity to blitz his opponent. If Red fails to roll a two next time, White can cover with any shot and should have clear sailing thereafter.

There is risk involved, of course. If Red rolls a two and White immediately rolls a one and subsequently can't get a six, Red may turn the game around. But the combination of all these factors occurring is far more remote than the possibility of Red making W2 and causing trouble for the rest of the game.

There was a lot of disagreement among the many spectators, and I'm not adamant about my suggested move. Once again this position demonstrates the healthy difference of opinion so rampant in backgammon.

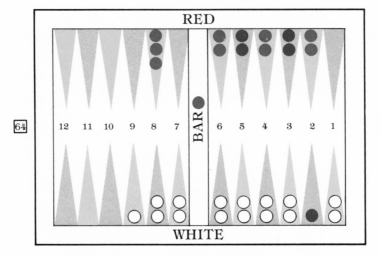

White to
play 4–3.
Red is
on the bar.